Stephen,

I, mentioned this book the other night at Faye's party. I
marked a couple of the poems that I like. I hope you enjoy it.

Russell Hiil

LAWYER POETS AND THAT WORLD WE CALL LAW

an anthology of poems about the practice of law

LAWYER POETS AND THAT WORLD WE CALL LAW

an anthology of poems about the practice of law

James R. Elkins
editor

Pleasure Boat Studio: A Literary Press
New York

Lawyer Poets and That World We Call Law
edited by James R. Elkins

ISBN 978-1-929355-97-6
Library of Congress Control Number: 2013907039
First U.S. Printing

Design and cover by Laura Tolkow

Pleasure Boat Studio is a literary press. Our books are available through your favorite bookstore and through SPD (Small Press Distribution), Partners/West, Baker & Taylor, Ingram, Brodart, Powells.com, Amazon.com, and bn.com,

and also through our website via credit card:
PLEASURE BOAT STUDIO: A LITERARY PRESS
www.pleasureboatstudio.com
201 West 89th Street
New York, NY 10024

Contact Jack Estes
Fax: 413-677-0085
Email: pleasboat@nyc.rr.com

Table Of Contents

Editor's Foreword

There are poets and there are lawyers. We think of them as residents of different worlds. In the bright light of day, the work of the lawyer seems to have absolutely nothing to do with that of the poet. The poet returns the favor: there is little need to try to imagine what it is lawyers do and how they do it. Two worlds, different enterprises, different ways of putting language to use.

Then, lo and behold, we learn that lawyers, in numbers more than astounding, turn out to be poets. Our poets are lawyers! Yes, some of them scribble doggerel, visited by a grey-robed muse of sentiment and sanctimony. Then, a bigger surprise: a surprising number of lawyers turn out to be excellent poets, taking their place in a history that can be traced to the first arrival of lawyers in America.

Most of the lawyer poets represented in this anthology are practicing lawyers (and judges); a few abandoned the legal profession to take up teaching and literary work. Unlike most lawyer poets who do not, in their poetry, lay claim to being lawyers and maintain a wall of separation between law and poetry, the poets in this anthology have been unable to remain silent in their poetry about the world in which they work. The lawyer poet who would disguise his tracks as a lawyer is one kind of poet. This anthology represents that rarer specimen, a poet who finds a place for the world of law in his poetry. For this rare species of poet lawyer, there's simply no walking away, no pretended separation, no divorce, and no compartmentalization of the world of the poem and the world of law. The poet knows both worlds, and thus is borne—legal verse.

Dedication

To the poets who know law—we now know there have been many,

to those who have chased the muse and abandoned the profession,

to those who stayed with the law and wrote poems at night,

to the poems we remember and the poets who made them,

to the poets whose poems will inevitably be forgotten,

to all, your poetry, fine and fumbling,

for it, and for you, these poems . . .

—James R. Elkins

Lawyer Poets and the Practice of Law

Tim Nolan

I write poetry and, from time to time, publish it. I also practice law. The two occupations are not always mutually exclusive. There are interesting moments when one discipline seeps into the other. There are other times when my dual interests could not seem further apart. During a prolonged and boring deposition a few months ago, my attention wandered out the window of the conference room to a hawk spiraling above the river bluffs with perfect grace and intention—making our lawyers' squabbles over construction change orders and contract interpretation seem remote and intensely silly. The poetry of the hawk's flight was obvious. The poetry of the stock phrase in an answer to a complaint— "Defendant is without knowledge or information sufficient to form a belief as to the truth of the matter, and, therefore, denies the same"—is less apparent.

Yet at the same time, I have come to value the precision and sense of a good legal argument—it is not unlike the argument of a good poem—quick, irrefutable and pressured by precedent. Lawyers cite to court opinions. Poets turn to Walt Whitman or Rainer Maria Rilke for precedent. The mind—sorting through history, memory, emotion, personal experience—ought to inform both poetry and the practice of law.

I have come to believe that there should be artfulness in the practice of law. Much of what a lawyer does involves creating something—an argument, a contract—where nothing existed before. The way in which a legal task is accomplished almost always involves compositional choices— how will the case be presented; how will the deal be structured? A lawyer is effective when he or she makes good compositional choices in a case and for a particular client. In litigating a lawsuit, a lawyer is often overwhelmed with facts, documents, statements, memories (good and bad), emotions, a hovering concept of justice (good and bad), time lines and time limits, bullet points and visual aids, practical and legal precedents, clients, judges, jurors. From all of this, the lawyer must draw out a story, with a cast of characters (sometimes stock characters), themes, compromises, and final outcomes. The good lawyer is able to not only marshal these various resources, but also draw out and suggest a final conclusion that serves his client. The poet, facing a blank piece of paper, has a similar task. From endless possibilities, what must be said? What words will be used to say it? What images will lend force to the words that are used? What kind of insight and mind will the music and sounds evoke?

For a lawyer or a poet, there are endless diversions, wrong ways, dead ends. Choices are innumerable. Possibilities, within the context of a case or a poem, seem infinite. Yet when the case is done, or the poem is written and rewritten (sometimes abandoned)—there is the same excitement: the next case, the next client, the next poem.

Readers of the poems in this anthology will be mindful of the stereotypes that we have of lawyers and of poets. Stereotypes serve a purpose. In a complex world, stereotypes help a person to categorize what is observed. Stereotypes also calm the mind and reassure a person that he knows what he does not know. The stereotype of the poet combines a number of easy attributes. The poet is a bohemian, irresponsible, free, flighty, subject to brilliant inspiration, aloof, poor, garroted, soulful, irreverent. The stereotype of the lawyer also involves easy attributes. The lawyer is masterful, composed, certain, needling, dogged, practical, insistent, combative, annoying, overdressed.

Stereotypes fall apart when applied to a single human being. The mask of the poet or mask of the lawyer are poor substitutes for the real human being and his collection of fear, joy, bewilderment, and experience. I find in Wallace Stevens, one of our most widely known lawyer-poets, a poet and a lawyer who came to appreciate in both his poetry and his work the similarities and differences of his two callings. Such recognition, no doubt hardwon, required him to be as alive and observant on his walks to work as he was when he arrived at his desk and his work as a lawyer and corporate executive for The Hartford Accident and Indemnity Company in Hartford, Connecticut, where he specialized in the intricacies of surety bonds on large construction projects.

Wallace Stevens understood that in both his poetry and his practice of law he was one human being trying to make subjective sense of what he "beheld." I do not believe that Stevens compartmentalized his life into literature and the law. He was a very good lawyer who also became one of our great poets. His work as a surety bond lawyer drew upon many of the same skills he had as a poet: intelligence, empathy, imagination, care. Wallace Stevens pushes us to rethink the stereotypes of lawyer and poet. Through the force of his personality and talent, Stevens was able to defy the stereotypes of both poet and lawyer to stand on ground of his own choosing.

For both a lawyer and a poet, the imagination must always be present. Wallace Stevens, in reviewing an insurance claim, used the same imagination at work in his poems to determine whether or not to pay the claim. Here is what a lawyer and poet must both be able to do: pick up a fact or image of nearly total insignificance—a mere marble along the way—and make it significant by the imaginative effort of paying attention. I am not advocating that lawyers or poets make up facts or images. Rather, I am saying that if the lawyer or the poet pays enough attention, he can learn that what seems insignificant hardly ever is, and, indeed, the outcome of the entire case, the meaning of the poem itself, may ultimately turn on it. I am a great believer in the Shakespearean maxim, "By indirections, find direction out." As a lawyer and a poet, my best work has been based on hunch and instinct. What might not initially seem to be a good approach, either legally or poetically, often ends up being the best possible approach, because it is my own.

Both poetry and the law involve the effort to move from fact to feeling, from observation to intuition. In a jury trial, how the lawyer presents his case is in some ways more important than what is presented. This is what drives the general public crazy about lawyers—how could they argue either side convincingly? What shamelessness! Lawyers know it is not difficult at all. A lawyer and a poet are both advocates. Accompanying this advocacy, there must be a generosity of spirit, a readiness to be empathetic. The lawyer must empathize with the client; the poet must have empathy with the reader.

There is intellectual malleability to both pursuits. As a lawyer, you can push facts and precedent around, or embrace them, or ignore them. You know there must be at least one jurist in some obscure court who thinks exactly as you do and supports your position. As a poet, you can push lines around, invent language, make the reader laugh or cry, speak in a voice that is yours or is imagined entirely. It is a mistake to think that the law is an objective hard-headed enterprise and poetry is for muddled-thinking romantics.

As I gather my thoughts here, a line hovers in the background— "Nothing that matters is a hobby." What I mean is that activities like law and poetry should be driven by the full human being, with full attention. When I tell people in my legal life that I write poetry, I sometimes see suspicion in their eyes. They assume that I write poetry as a pastime or hobby, as if it is interchangeable with needlepoint or bowling. I want to say, "No. You don't understand."

As lawyers, we should be open to the world as we develop empathy for our clients and their situations. At the same time, we must be attuned to our own passions and remain agents of curiosity in our profession. Whenever a potential client tells me they want me to be a "pit bull," I tell them I'm a diligent and eager golden retriever, and they probably do not really want a pit bull, because pit bulls tend to bite everyone, even clients.

Whatever the public might think of lawyers as a group or however often the mistaken stereotype is advanced, we should work to defy the stereotype. I urge you to create something other than footnotes in legal briefs. Write poetry. Sing opera. Play the drums. Not just for therapy. Or to pass the time. Or to save yourself for your work as a lawyer. Do whatever it is because you must. You must. You have no choice.

There may be nothing more to say to my colleagues who are suspicious and skeptical about poetry, no argument that will overcome their resistance to the idea that poetry might matter. What I can do for those who remain curious is to offer the poems compiled by Jim Elkins presented in this anthology.

A Lawyer's Education

WHAT THE LAW IS

Lee Warner Brooks

"The law …," the law professor paused, as if
Amazed…, "Do you know what the law is? Eh?"
He paused again, as if poised on a cliff
From which he spied—arriving all the way

From Magna Carta, like the nick of white
A sail makes when its hull has sunken past
The sea's horizon—ocean waves in tight,
Winddriven rows, all lunarwoven fast

Together—interyarned in unison
By physics too complex to calculate
In alphabetics, but whose metrics run
Inerrantly to shore. He didn't wait

For us to answer—or for tide to ebb—
"The law," he told us, "is a seamless web."

LAW SCHOOL

James McKenna

Late each night
at my desk, window dark,
cases were read and notes
taken. Ideas marched
by in the lamp's steady beam
until they seemed
shining, heedless armies.
Then switch off the light.
The street springs to sight:
ragged walkers, limping,
arms, faces lashed,
as though in retreat from
some hopeless class.

HADLEY V. BAXENDALE (1854)

James McKenna

At 23 we quickly married, then
straight to law school, night division.
It was work, school, study.
We kept our heads down.
But Saturdays we studied together.
This Saturday in the Library of Congress,
its small, somber law rooms.
She's taking down *Corbin on Contracts*
and sees me watching.
I'm outlining damages,
the foreseeability of reasonable men,
and feel her staring.
We start to laugh and cannot stop.
She flees to the stacks.
I change tables.
She piles books and ducks her head.
I try holding my breath.
Nothing works.
How could we have known.

LAW SCHOOL

Ace Boggess

Prof. McLaughlin often told me
I would have a chair at the law school
named in my honor:
not a Chair, endowed for a seat
on the faculty or for scholarship;
a physical chair—umber-
tinged & sallow-banded
like striations on the peeled side
of a mountain—the seat where
I spent afternoons
watching lawyers-in-waiting
shuffle down a hall toward the library,
heavy packs of dread on their backs.
I kept my place in the lounge,
listened for arguments featuring
misquotes from the Bible & Sun Tzu.
I inhaled rich perfume,
ghost scents of cigar smoke.
I laughed, waited, let the conversations
come to me.
Journal in hand, I took notes
on the note-takers,
joining their loneliness
when I could. To keep safe,
I had the chair in which I wrote &
dreamt with well-lit eyes:
I picture Wallace Stevens
in law school, safe & happy

searching women
through to the World Soul,
or in the proper
study of Mankind
engaging his imagination
on a frolic of his own.

HERR DOKTOR

Charles Williams

The Finality of Homicide

Herr Doktor of Criminal Law
has sprouted his own Sonny Bono moustache.
30 years old, 5'10", 175 pounds,
he has pleasant, but menacing, brown eyes.

His heavy black eyebrows twink
when he lectures on the derelicts
who get their names into these cases.
Instead of "homicide,"
he writes "homocide" on the board.
I wonder if Mein Herr
has unconscious gay issues, or any issues—
So much for that—I'm quitting his class.
He can't spell!

Ode to Wilburt Hamm

Herr Doktor of Contracts
is a kind gentleman
with fine twinkling blue eyes.
He loves to ask questions
of common sense and facts.
Unlike other classes,
I know the answers here.
They're all just common sense,

nothing ethereal
or things procedural.
"But did you purchase it?"
"And did you know of it?"
"And how and where and when?"
I like Hamm's class the best.

Res Ipsa Loquitur

Herr Doktor of Torts talks like a duck.
He speaks through his platapine nose.
He instructs us of Boodle's barrels,
how they rolled from above into a street.
Barrels in a street, we are to suppose,
have no explanation that's neat.
The Chancellor held "Res Ipsa"—
"Res Ipsa Loquitur," which means:
"The thing (always) quacks for itself."
And so does our fine Herr Doktor.

Civil Procedure

Herr Doktor of Civil Procedure
preaches like Jonathan Edwards
(and takes about as long).
Sinners in the hands of an angry God
are nothing compared to poor law students
in the grasp of an angry Professor.
His classes in Civil Procedure
verge toward their own eternity,
and spark my own divine contemplations
of unending, precise damnations.

Dante foresees a frozen lake of pain—
as cold as the Court's holding in
Palsgraf versus The Long Island Railroad?
Our Baptists believe in a Hell that's hot,
a boiling cauldron of sulphur and steam,
which brings me to the obvious question:
Is Hell hot or is it cold?
I'd say, for now, it's neither—
Hell is a class in Civil Procedure.

The Rule in Shelley's Case

Herr Doktor of Property recites
the Rule in Shelley's Case.
He says it has confounded
jurists for hundreds of years.
But the Rule in Shelley's Case is simple.
Any farmer (like me) understands it:
the Earth outlasts the wills of men.

Epilogue

The conceits of the law professor
are
cryptically
endless,
endlessly
cryptic.

AFTER 60 DAYS OF SNOW ON THE GROUND

Charles Williams

> —for Robert Lawson, who taught Evidence,
> and noticed birds singing outside in the thaw,
> after long snow cover

Snow retreats and mist arises,

four robins hopping

as if on dew.

DISCOVERY IN LAW SCHOOL

Charles Williams

Today I offered myself
to what is left
of myself
and found
inside my soul
two yellow and white puppy dogs,
neargrown, and playful
as the shifting colors
of a new Spring dawn.
To one in Law School at thirty,
a most satisfying discovery.

WE ARE ALL BORN LAWLESS AS DOGS

Charles Williams

Spring is the tiller of the soul—
That deepest look within the folds
Where East is Vajra
And West is Law,
And all men ought to know
That they are born lawless as dogs.

LAW

James Clarke

Law is
a small fire
in a clearing
at night
spilling warmth
& light

But,
step too close
& the blaze
will shock you
cold in your tracks,
give you a chill.

ALL IN A DAY'S WORK

WHITE SHIRT

David Bristol

Blue, pink, ecru,
stripes narrow and bold, red and green,
now waking, wanting a white shirt.
Quiet and simple,
shunned for lack of style, color.

The simple is sought,
sparse and absolute to wear for the day.
Clean, white, lightly starched
and unremarkable,
a modest gesture of presentment.

Step plainly, showing a humble color,
out of the house
washed.

THE TIE I NEVER WORE TO WORK

Richard Bank

Hand painted iridescent pheasant wings flash above the tall grass.
The wide and shortened shape reveals its hoary thrift-shop age.
The bird breaks, evokes red shotgun shells on a cabin shelf or
a vision of pristine wilderness fluttering on painted silk.

In the dour courthouse where uniforms fill the hallways,
the killer glocks are cased and sleeping; respectful and benign.
My tie was power red, long and smooth; modest and professional.
To the clients, I was the wizard, ready to chant and throw the runes.

Early hour of rising now shines and glows with peace and coffee.
Suits and dress shirts fill the quiet chambers of the closets;
the scuffed and battered briefcase of war holds briefs no more.
I pull down my hat, set out into the airy, welcoming universe.

IN THE OFFICE OF AN ATTORNEY SPECIALIZING IN ACCIDENT CASES

David Leightty

Ranked on his shelf are lawbooks—poised, replete.
Below, there blares the racket of the street.

OFF THE RECORD

David Leightty

—young attorney at a multiparty deposition

Witness, that small wraith of the air.

Deponents sworn to solemn truth
Authenticated *what* and *whom*.
But questions, answers dimmed; his stare
meandered the appointed room.

Then he divined a finer proof—
Perched an arm's length outside the glaze
Thirty floors up, a sparrow hawk:
Bright copper mantle; robin size
But with the fierce square raptor face;
Alert through bold, dark facial marks.

Call it out? Not in that sober forum,
Good judgment swayed by sheer decorum.

THE LAWYER'S DAILY TIME LOG

Jesse Mountjoy

7:00 a.m. Shave, look in mirror
For signs of noncompliance with
The Federal Possibilities Act
(Nonbillable).

7:40 a.m. Drive to office; thoughts
Re: first principles of ambiguity
(Nonbillable).

8:15 a.m. Research statutes
(the tingle of a law book's spine)
Re: application of rule against perpetuities
To unborn children;
Analysis of dreams of bureaucrats.

9:30 a.m. Preparation of waivers
And consents for election of directors.
Attend nonexistent meeting of Board
Of Directors of dissolved company.

Noon. Luncheon meeting
With deceased client re: moral flaws
Of intestate succession; review of,
And revisions to, Last Will.

2 p.m. Review of premarital contract
Specifically Article IV (Representations)
Re: either party's past devotion

To Dante's Beatrice (or Proust's Albertine).
Prioritize the order of past marriages
And future passions.

4 p.m. Conference call with clients
Re: obscure laws of association
From enigmatic words handwritten
On back of stained wine list;
Amputation of oaths before a notary public.

5:30 p.m. Sit at desk. Recite the mantra
"Time is of the essence"; review
Various abbreviated forms of eternity;

Attempts to contact Kant's fellow legislators
In the kingdom of ends.

6:30 p.m. Drive home to some
Final unaccountable justice
(Nonbillable).

DRIVING TO A TAX SEMINAR, NOTRE DAME, INDIANA

Jesse Mountjoy

The dry gold of late September corn.
Stalks stiffbacked, moral.
Fields of soybeans, alfalfa, fescue.
The offwhite, light grey of silos and grainbins.
Dusk the color of molten lead.
All in transition from one shade,
One tonality, to another.
Flat, straight Highway 31
With no margin of error granted to explorers,
Up through and out of Kokomo,
Safe behind my windshield,
On to towns to the north with
South American names:
Peru, Mexico, LaPaz—Indiana.
The farmhouses are asleep
With fitful dreams of lying awake
And watching my Jeep drive past,
And of listening for the fields.
For there are words buried in them
As deep as last century's plow bits.
Lost solemn words, grey bearded words,
Shaken and fallen from ancient books
With ivory covers
And tarnished metal clasps,
Kept and fondled by great-aunts of the Midwest.
The words wait to heal the new silences,
To be repeated endlessly

By Alzheimer patients
Or teenagers racing to the varsity game.
The words wait to surface
After a late harvest.
They wait for me to drive south
Through these heartland counties
Where the innocence of habit
Wrestles daily with the malicious divinities
Of law and passion
Behind the shadows of barns,
Where the darkening horizon
Enters the earth and gives birth
To a posthumous world.

LAST DAY OF THE YEAR

Jesse Mountjoy

Last day of the year,
Driving to the Capitol from western Kentucky
For some final corporate filings.
The luxury of clear roads
And early morning rests on my eyelids
Until a few miles east of Elizabethtown
Toward the New Haven exit,
In opalescent pockets of fog
I see the cliff's shadows
Like stoopshouldered old men
Reserving austerity to themselves,
And the ice hidden by blown snow.
I catch the late moon in my throat,
My stomach an alembic of sparrows
And think for some reason
Of William Carlos Williams's
> *No one*
> *to witness*
> *and adjust, no one to drive the car*
And travel like a trumpet
Touching at times on the right notes,
Over a score by Hummel,
With a prayer, not for certainty,
But for the postponement of uncertainty,
Brakeless and finally alive in the thin light.

WORK

Tim Nolan

On Monday, I am optimistic.
I can push a mountain of paper
off my desk and into the trash.
Those notes I kept six months ago
will remind me to call that guy
in Florida who wants to dodge
a bullet. The letter I write
on Tuesday will assure
the State that iron ore
in a boxcar in Duluth was only
temporarily resident on January 1.

The judge who loves me will issue
an order granting me lifetime
good health, wealth, happy children.
Let Judgment Be Entered Accordingly.

By midweek, I have put off lunch again.
I am stalled over a crossword puzzle.
My best intentions are focused on
39 DOWN—"Artfully shy" three letters
ending in "y." By Thursday,

I have put off enough for one week.
A client refuses to tell me who his
employer is. "It's a matter
of national security." He's not even
kidding. He gives me the number

for the FBI. If I don't believe him.

By Friday, I have billed myself out.
I have nothing left to say.
The spring light falls long
on my shoulders. I can see the river
from here. The ice has broken. Gone south.

"Coy" was the word. "Artfully shy."
Or was it "artfully sly"?
Who cares? The week is wrapped
in brown paper and waxed parcel string.

OKLAHOMA

Tim Nolan

I thought it would be dry and cattle-driven,
but Oklahoma is green, almost Irish.
Down the interstate in my rental car,
I see cattle grazing in the thick brush.

I am here on business to meet a man
who used to make hearing aids, and now
trains rodeo horses. In this country,
we can change ourselves overnight.

I am here to find out if the man
will be a good witness at a trial.
I am stage manager of his memory and belief,
midwife of testimony favorable to my side.

He's late. I wait at the Lazy E Ranch—
an "E" sloping sideways down a hill.
I am sloping sideways half the time,
my head full of hearing aid history.

Beneath an oak tree on a hill, I smoke
and watch rodeo calves and bulls
grazing in their time. In Minnesota
this morning, I felt the first snap

of winter, that chill breath at dawn,
the long struggle about to begin. Now,
I'm kicking red dust from my boots.

I've never seen such red hot soil!
The Florida Seminole tribe was sent here
during the presidency of Andrew Jackson
in the first long march across the land.
Oklahoma was the frontier no one wanted.

My witness is here. He is perfect.
The jury will think he's Gary Cooper,
speaking in measured, confident sentences.
He says exactly what I'd hoped he'd say.

As we speak, sitting side-by-side
in a Lazy E Golf cart, a mottled calf
shoots out of a cage into the corral,
kicking up red dust, panicked.

The soon-to-be, next greatest, champion
cowboy horse bolts after, hooves clattering,
leather snapping, the bright and stiff rope
cinches, the poor calf drops. Everything

suddenly stops. It is so strange
to fly down through the bell of the country
to arrive at a time and place where
archetypes stall. The pursued are caught.

At Will Rogers World Airport, I buy
a refrigerator magnet in the shape
of Oklahoma wearing an oil well and a war bonnet.
A Seminole woman waits for a flight to Detroit.
She should be flying back to Florida
to reclaim her land and place.

But it's more complicated than that. At the airport
in Memphis, Elvis is everywhere, alive, doing

alright, transcending himself, ascending
into hyper space where he breathes
the pure vapor of our collected departures.
I can't hear a thing. Stunned, as usual, in flight.

SILENCES

Lee Warner Brooks

Lawyers learn to listen to what wasn't
said—as well as how to not say what
should not be said; a ready wit that doesn't
aid your case is best kept quiet. But

this cannot mean a colloquy of lawyers
can be silent—we by nature speak
incessantly—because as legal warriors
whose sole weapon is the word, we seek

to quiet silences that might sustain
an inconvenient fact or contradiction—
so we speak—but, speaking, we refrain
from any sound that could give rise to friction

with our theory of the case—our way
of saying what we're careful not to say.

THE RULES OF EVIDENCE

Lee Robinson

What you want to say most
is inadmissible.
Say it anyway.
Say it again.
What they tell you is irrelevant
can't be denied and will
eventually be heard.
Every question
is a leading question.
Ask it anyway, then expect
what you won't get.
There is no such thing
as the original
so you'll have to make do
with a reasonable facsimile.
The history of the world
is hearsay. Hear it.
The whole truth
is unspeakable
and nothing but the truth
is a lie.
I swear this.
My oath is a kiss.
I swear
by everything
incredible.

GROUNDS FOR DIVORCE

Lee Robinson

These are our grounds,
says the lawyer, as if
they could share this grief.
The client's eyes find the window
behind his bobbing head.

First, adultery:
Out there, a garden of delights,
everything green, about
to flower. Primitive, Rousseau.
Eve sings to the snake and neither
cares about Adam,
who is this fellow in the threepiece suit,
this lawyer lecturing.

Physical cruelty, he says,
is difficult to prove.
A sudden tempest blows the window shut.
Rain beats the glass.
We'll need to show repeated abuse, or short
of that, a life-threatening attack.
Outside, in what was once
the garden, wind rips the grass from its roots,
sucks whole trees into the sky. Afterwards,
the bruised earth sleeps and for mile after mile
there is nothing but loss, like the eerie streets
of de Chirico.

Habitual drunkenness, he continues,
hissing the last syllable,
includes drug abuse. His eyebrows
rise into question marks. Are you hot?
I'll open the window.
Below, on the bench in the littered
park, a wino drains the last of his wine,
throws the bottle into the street.
At the sound of glass splintering
she is her schoolgirl self again,
the smallest one
in the group at the museum, faint
at the sight of the absinthe drinker's face.
Now, he says, I've saved the easiest
for last. It's what we call 'no fault'—
a year without cohabitation.

He checks his notes, the form
she filled out in the waiting room.
Looks like we're almost there!
Through the window she can see
the sign blinking from the restaurant:
Open. Inside, she is the only customer,
a figure more alone
than even Hopper could imagine.
There she will wait for the year to be over.
The waiter looks oddly like her lawyer.
He fills her coffee cup and takes her money.
She knows without asking
he doesn't want to hear her story.

FAMILY LAW

Kristen Roedell

I.
There are as many lawyer jokes
as embroidered aprons
at a church bazaar, or Hershey bars
at an AA meeting, or crows
in my neighbor's yard.
People tell me these jokes.
I say: *"everyone hates a lawyer*
until he needs one,"
which produces the sort of
silence during which I fill out
a retainer contract.

II.
Clients see the group toy box
under my receptionist's desk,
her tender smile,
the framed photo of my daughter,
and they feel I understand.
I do understand, but phone
slips pile up so tall on my desk
that the paperweight mouse gives up,
and I have to peel out
in the daycare parking lot
to arrive at court on time.

III.
To the ones who call daily

to recount visitation arguments,
(the fact that ears were pierced,
and gerbils purchased
to win affections), I say:
"It's $20 every time I pick this phone up."

This puts perspective
on how the child's laundry was returned,
how much sugar was given
to a hypoglycemic seven-year-old,
and whether entertainment
was PG-13.

IV.
Eventually, homemade fudge
in plastic wrap
no longer arrives at my office.
The children have already
seen all the toys,
the other lawyer has a better suit,
and his file is color-coded.
The statement from my office
goes over 30 days.

When the trial date arrives both sides
have found other relationships.
They are tired of meeting at Burger King
as neutral territory
when children are exchanged.
The judge splits the baby,
which the next door neighbor
could have predicted.

V.
At last, the client makes
his final fee payment.
He says, during this visit,
"This is how you lawyers all get rich."
I tell my favorite lawyer joke,
the one about the 500 dead lawyers.

Then, I take out the office garbage,
tie my Volvo door shut with twine,
and peel out towards the
daycare parking lot.

WHAT PERSISTS IN RISING

Kristen Roedell

My office was down an alleyway,
pebbled and uneven as the path
to a French grocer's;
the building clung like a limpet
on the hillside.
Fall Street was tarred,
growing sticky in the summers
when the heat rose;
on the south side
the courthouse ruminated.
Big Firm Lawyers crossed over like jockeys
astride brisk, burnished arguments,
their briefcases as tack,
clients hanging on tails.
The sole-practitioners followed
without patina, listing to starboard
with boxes of files.
My clients strung along behind me
carrying children
with gum in their hair.

In a hot June, my maternity dress
hung in thick folds,
when even my cat knew
to shed her winter fur.
In another county,
my own divorce grew as hot
as the road past the courthouse,

while my daughter moved in me
like a ball of yarn unspooling.
She was the child of my old age,
flung as a rope from a departing ship.
I took the shape of a spinnaker
flush in a Northern wind.

There was a rhythm to my work,
the courtroom dividing moons,
crescents coming and going.
In October, the Japanese Maples crisped;
Judges began to hesitate,
wincing as I argued my cases
bent backwards like the last
match in a book.
My clients wore a look of shame
and bravado, and I made apologies
to balustrades when brushing by.
I balanced with the grace
of an olive on toothpicks
while ice grew in spider webs
making lace on the courthouse steps.

When January came,
I could no longer make a date
in court. Cars slid on Fall Street,
my heels making holes
in pavement slush.
Snow rushed in gutters
confounding the storm drains;
wind unfurled coats
picking briefcase locks.

I gave in to my belly
and held my tongue,
as women do.

These sixteen years
I have not thought of this,
until today; I drove by
in the gold season of Fall Street.
You turned your elegant face
towards halls where files are shuffled,
their cases still called.
It remains an enigma
how something so fair
persists in rising
from sorrow.

SLIP AND FALL LAWYER

Carl Reisman

I am becoming
an acolyte of the slip
and fall;
slips on water,
over concrete blocks,
on icy walks. My family
fed by falls.

The moment of panic
when the biped is poised
between
air and earth,
the terrible nostalgia
of gravity.

I pick up the pieces,
plead bad acts.

When I close my eyes
I see an endless
procession of slips,
a flurry of plaintiffs
tumbling from the sky,
wide-eyed in their
innocence.

SLIP & FALL

Rachel Contreni Flynn

To guard against it, the grocery stores
put plastic mats in the produce aisles
with holes the approximate size and shape
of the typical grape. I'm talking about liability.
I'm talking about avoiding the awful snap
of collarbone on linoleum, the shatter
of graham crackers and bifocal glasses.

I've been worried about the birds I cut
from construction paper that didn't look
like birds but anvils or trowels. Anyway
they did the job. Fewer bloody splotches
against the glass, fewer reasons to feel guilty
for getting in the way of hunger and abject
joy. I've been lost in the oil slick

of a junco's wing. I'm dark and sticky with it,
but regardless, all day I've been singing a poem
about traveling, singing even as I reach
for the phone to talk about insurance and risk
and plausible options, singing even though
everything I dream these nights is forests
and hands and bones and the winter rattles me.

It's a song about the end of caution—
an onyx pendant slipping from my neck
and smashing on the supermarket's asphalt
where gulls are painted to ward off

a mess. But harm is not worth avoiding
if the cure is smallness . . . . I wheel gladly beyond it
to the hole in the sky where birds are spiraling.

POEM ON THE ROAD TO DEPOSE

Rachel Contreni Flynn

My body is a sack
of black spoons,
and my dreams
steal from me.

My books are full
of bite marks.

The lights outside Milwaukee falter—
good morning, corpse candles.

I've come zealously to represent
my client and will not listen

to the click
of the black spoons.

Purified by diesel
and the long gray bone
of the sky,

I am limbcaught and swallowed
by the monstrous laws of the dead.

FELONY WAIVERS

Richard Bank

The bail people come up to talk.
The teenager who sold to a narc is with his mom.
She doesn't believe the mandatory sentence.
The girlfriend who called the cops
Now wants to drop the case.

The graying man in the tie and alligator shoes
Caught carrying a gun in a bar
Has that 8:30 AM vodka smell.
His record is old but long,
He knows what conviction means.

The DA makes offers, asks for stipulations;
Drug scans, ballistics, accident reports.
The schitzing crack whore in the cell-room
Gets a program for a plea to obstructing.
Both retail thieves go home.

I put on two car thefts and the direct sale,
The suppression in the gun case
Is held under advisement
And the domestic is put out six months
For no further problems.

The room empties out,
The day draws to a close.
The DA and the steno compare engagement rings,
The sheriff locks the cell-room door,
Court stands adjourned.

DOING LINEUPS ON MY BIRTHDAY

Richard Bank

First you flew over the jungle canopy,
your chopper throbbing like a heart.
I was in the movement, striving against it all.

We crossed swords in the frenetic courtroom,
you in high boots and fifty mission crush
describing how blood glistens on the dull
3:00 a.m. streets as if it were alive and I,
asking the time between the call and arrest,
radio descriptions, the cuffed I.D.
The jurors saw you as an Oracle, girded for war.

Now I am the technocrat, filing motions,
attending pre-trial conferences in a bow tie;
you are detailed to the prison, running lineups.
We talk about statistics, the per diem for a cell,
that our paths have suddenly crossed again when
the phone announces your second grandchild,
born on my birthday far from this gray place.

Somehow, I felt all along that neither of us
ever wanted more than home.

MY CLIENT

John Levy

who committed his crime
drunk and then, still
drunk, confessed to the police
is angry

that he was indicted, keeps
telling me that someone else who did
something much worse
got off "scotch free."

The last thing he needs to
hear is
his vocabulary is also
in deep shit.

PREMEDITATED, DELIBERATED & INTENTIONAL

Richard Krech

After three days the jury came back
with its verdict: guilty of murder
w/special circumstances.
A month later
we sit here again,
waiting for the penalty phase verdict.
The jury not only deliberating
my client's fate this time,
but their own as well:
will they too be guilty of murder?

Premeditated murder this time.
Not the rash impulsive act of a teenager
but the sober calculated decision
of 12 adults:
a teacher, a fireman, a nurse . . .
Not my client's peers
by any stretch of the imagination.

The prosecutor having removed all blacks
from the jury
over my objection
and w/the court's blessing.

Will they cast the second stone?

PLEA BARGAIN, JUNE 29

M.C. Bruce

I'm waking from the early afternoon,
I watch the trees outside nod with the wind.
I need to go and plead a client soon.

The café radio casts out a tune,
a lover's plea: Forgive him, he has sinned.
I'm waking from the early afternoon

to reappear and try to staunch the wound
of a life beneath the law now pinned.
I need to go and plead a client soon.

Outside the vagary of testy June,
the sun in pale blue sky, alone and skinned.
I'm waking from the early afternoon,

the taste of sleep now fading. Here, the moon
has come out early, shaking white and thinned.
I need to go and plead a client soon.

The letter of the law reads like a rune.
"This'll be quick," the good bailiff grinned.
I've wakened from the early afternoon.
My client slumps. He'll be pleading soon.

SETTLING ON THE EVE OF TRIAL

Joyce Meyers

So it's over. I wash off
the war paint, stow
my weapons, go home
and have a glass of wine.

After two years of full speed
ahead, a wild roller coaster ride,
someone pulls the switch
just before the final plunge

and leaves me stranded,
suspended, my body tightly
coiled, ready to spring.
Somewhere in the far

distance a fog descends
on truth, and justice sways
in the breeze. I await
the slow uncoiling.

LEGAL AID

Susan Holahan

Client with beautiful hands clutching baby said as she sat down,
"I don't know how the shit I got me into such a mess like this. I got to
get me some money somewhere down the line." I said I'd take her down
to City because they have to keep her going while she's off State. As we
drove, client said she worked two months and didn't tell State. Worse, they
found out she signed to buy a house with the father of her first three kids.
Someone told State and State threatened to discontinue her. Now the
father was gone. Before he left he sold the house to his mother *for a dollar*.
State discontinued client, but she and the kids kept on. The baby wanted a
bottle, didn't understand she was supposed to discontinue. We stopped on
office time for milk, on the way to City.

Client and baby wrestled in the hard, dirty chairs chained down in
the waiting room while the front desk told me the supervisor gave client
appointment for next week, Don't bother him.

Supervisor said he couldn't do a thing. "Look at the statute," I said.
"Statute says *shall*. You *have* to give her something."

"These people make so many problems for themselves," he said. He
took the papers inside, finally. Came out beaming: "We won!"

I collected client and baby. In another two hours we were out in the
wet afternoon with the food voucher. The worker fixed it so client had to
go all the way to Big Buy instead of Sam's Corner Market down her block.
More economical, he said, you *must* know someone with a car.

"Sometimes your clients don't tell you everything that's going on."
The worker at State slid me a checking glance. I waited for the report he
should have sent weeks ago on the client with the hands, the one they
discontinued because the father of some of her kids sold the house
she lived in to his mother *for a dollar*. We needed State's report
before the next hearing. "There was property in this case. Look at
that: 'Discontinuance due to disposal of property.' She had a house,

and she disposed of it. She can't do that without telling us. That's against the rules." This worker had a face like a very old apple. He looked across the room and shook his head. "I been around a long time. Crazy system." He went out again. "The file isn't there," he said when he came back. "What I'm going to say when I write it up is 'Discontinued due to disposal of property.' On this issue you're cooked. What I would do if I was you, I'd talk to my client, person to person, between now and the hearing. Get her conned. Find out exactly what's been going on. Maybe she disposed of this property; but now she hasn't got a dime and she has four kids to feed. A reapplication, see what I mean?" The apple bobbed at me indulgently. "You Legal Aid people. You mean well. But you haven't been around as long as I have. Con your client good. Then, maybe if the file turns up, I'll give you a call before Wednesday."

This client has fingertips chewed down to blood spots. She gets passed on to someone new after each staff meeting on Client Dependency. First time she got me she needed an emergency food voucher: City had cut her off on a fraud charge. I picked up the phone; ten minutes and she had her food voucher. Next time she called they were trying to get her on Disability. "I'm not taking any of their shit. Disability. *They're* crazy to think I'll go for that—" and why is everybody after her? I stalled. She told me to go fuck myself. I hung up. Phone rang again. "I say what comes into my head and somebody gets mad, but I didn't mean to hurt you." Next they were throwing her out of her apartment. "That's an emergency, isn't it?—if you can only take emergencies?" Then her landlord was after her dogs and cats. Somebody was beating them to get rid of her. A lawyer felt sorry for client until the ASPCA inspector said *client* beats the animals. Better than beating children, I said. Client has no children, lawyer said.

Client calls every day now around lunchtime: NO FOOD. City has her checks for two months right in the office, but she missed an appointment. Head lawyer says not to worry: client gets fed by people who were in the hospital with her. But here she is, hungry. "All you have to do is pick up a phone, they listen to you. You won't help me because I'm white. It's completely fucked up. They cut me off again. I'm out on the street. Do something!"

"We can't take ..."

"This *is* an emergency."

"Not by our rules."

"Isn't this Legal Aid, where you help people for free?"

"Still free. We just don't help anybody."

"I can't go down there again."

"Sit with it. Talk quietly. Don't let them make you angry."

"They're trying."

"No one's trying to get *you*. It's the same for everyone. A fucked-up system"—I'm actually saying this—"the only one we have."

"Being treated this way makes me sick to my stomach."

I have been watching people cry in my office. City *has to* aid any person who "belongs to the town." This person belongs to the town. I shrug, "Maybe they *are* out to get you. Let's get over there. We'll get you. Something. Food. Or money." City is across town, next to a pool hall, right under State. The whole place clatters. Along the walls above the benches are blotches where heads rest. We don't even have an appointment. I better comb our hair.

FOUND OBJECTS

Lawrence Russ

A novice lawyer, I was sent
with a case full of papers
to the famous attorney.

In a tower with white
marble facing,
tens of stories above the ground,
he talked and talked on the phone
while I waited

on the far other side
of his burled desk.
The man who represented judges
and churches, baseball players and banks

made his wishes known.
His voice would circle, lift, and glide,
then twist
and clench,
as he stirred, then savored
men's envy, men's hate.

But how had his regular features grown
so misshapen, so lumpish,
his cheeks and brows
unevenly swollen, his skin
dull and wrinkled,
or shiny and tight, by turns.

As though someone had beaten him
daily, for weeks.

Between us, the surface
of his huge desk swirled
with glazed, luxurious
reds and browns.

Meant to resemble a glamorous desert,
it was empty, except
for two lucite cubes
that faced the visitors' chairs:

In the one, an infant rattlesnake,
expertly stuffed,
reared up,
its shiny length coiled,
its head cocked back, its hollow
fangs extended.

In the other, a three-inch scorpion
reached out
with serrated pincers.
Its hinged black tail
arched over its back,
the needle tip pointing downward, as if
at any moment, it might

pierce its own armored head
with poison.

THE EAGLE

Steven M. Richman

We discussed several commas
in the press of deadlines.
It has come down to this,
after all the facts and argument,
over where to place a comma.

Sauber, in his Italian suit
and silk tie, hair slicked back,
speaking quickly as if to outrace
the hourly rates he charges,
pounds the table. It has become
a point of principle, affecting
the integrity of the past week
of work.

Days later, in court, he will
drive home his point and note
with a self-satisfied smile
the judge's reaction. Convinced
of the sanctity of the written
word as he has written it,
he will soar into a thought
beyond the words, seeking
solace in the grammar and punctuation
of terms defined by someone else,
like a captured eagle seeking
within the confines of an aviary
to pretend that the cliffs are endless,

that the hunt still matters, forgetting
the crucial difference between survival
and surviving.

THE FIFTH WATCH OF THE NIGHT

Steven M. Richman

Sauber, Esq., is practicing his argument.
The small clock glows green by his bedside.
It is no longer the Sung Dynasty, he knows,
and his own boyhood is a thing escaped, lost
to the vagaries of shifted river beds. No,
there is no regaining it, a thing gone.
Books once read, characters understood, all gone,
gathering dust. Mrs. Sauber sleeps peacefully
on her left side. Bad for the heart,
Sauber knows, and, secure in his advocacy,
glimpses the faintest nipple-pink glimmerings of dawn,
and smiles.

Such things survive even the hail of missiles
and sprouting mushrooms. Has this been a dream?
True, it rained the night before, or was it tonight?
Worms cover the sidewalk. It is chilly
and his neighbors are all retrieving newspapers,
oblivious to the silent dissonance of light
in the cloud-streaked, sun-naked morning sky.
Droplets of water still cling to dandelions
on the fresh-cut suburban lawns.

Sauber keeps watch these last two hours,
noting the zeppelin-like filaments of cloud,
the snoring of Mrs. Sauber, the anticipation

of court; and prays to shooting stars
in language long discarded, prayers and stars
only viscerally seen and vicariously traveled.

THE THRILL OF THE HUNT, THE MOMENT OF THE KILL

Bruce Laxalt

Credentialed, thrice gowned,
Oft published, renowned,
And now for the pre-trial price of six hundred an hour,
I've purchased the privilege of hearing your deposition indictment
Of my apparently inept and callous client,
Hurled with arrogant elan from the towers of academe
    like an erudite bolt:
Fifty years of corporate design engineering for apparent naught,
Except to kill a careless but earnest working man
With a defective machine that even your graduate students
Could criticize with academic ease.

Respectfully always, almost shyly at first,
I query with deference on your magnificent C.V.
In awe, a bit, I must appear to you,
Another student, perhaps. Understandably nervous
    in the presence of the master.
Explain that term to me, Sir. I don't quite . . .
I didn't understand that concept, Professor, until today.

And then, slowly, we begin the dance into the forest.
Spins of logic, gentle repartee, far indeed from the expected
    harsh melee,
As you teach your unexpected and delightful new pupil
    the principles of the science.
No, the art of the science in your practiced hands,
Oblivious in the heady glow of your seduction
To the quiet fact that you are not leading this dance:

Well, didn't you write about that in 1985, Sir?

Do you still agree with your article that said . . .
Of course I do, you say with a benevolent smile.
And that article makes the point we were discussing.
And then, a shiver, I can see it pass through you.
Too late it begins to dawn that I am too facile by half
    with the arcane terms.
Too late the faint thought that I quote your articles,
Am familiar, somehow, with those of your less egotistical peers,
Too late the vague but rising feeling, nothing more than that yet,
That, even at your side, I've been stalking you
On your majestic and graceful walk through the woods.

And then, the millisecond when the three dimensions
    fall away like shattered ice,
And you know we are alone as you have never been.
And you look through my eyes, to see that I am
    seeing through yours,
And that you are where I've wanted you to be,
Cemented in the stone of the sworn record to simple truths
    you cannot square
With the mercenary condemnation of my client
We haven't even begun yet to discuss,
And that no one knows it yet but we two.
You are indeed the proudest of champions, Professor.
And only you and I know that you are slain.

Appearances and etiquette are important, we both agree,
And we do the final processional hand in hand:
I listen respectfully to your scholarly assault on my client's
    dangerous and defective design,

Given now with a haunted hunted look in your eyes.
I am not so petty as to probe or haggle or contradict.
There will be time for that in trial, we both know well.
And you are thinking that even Rommel fell prey
    to his vainly published ego,
And, imperiled to the edge of ruin,
Could not cast it away in time to save his army.

The chairs pushed back, the briefcases closed,
The sworn record's tension dispelled like mist.
So thank you, Professor. It's been an honor and a pleasure.
We'll see each other again, I trust, at time of trial?
Or, my eyes say to you above my smile and handshake,
Should you have a later quiet word with the inattentive vandal
Who retained you as his champion, and then sat deaf-eared
    while you fell in battle.
These cases can and should be resolved, you know.
And all can walk away head-high, the victory claimed.
Or, Professor, instead, shall you stand exposed,
The whore denounced,
The con man revealed,
Alone in the medieval marketplace of the courtroom,
With rank coin the measure of your academic virtue.

MIDNIGHT AT THE LAW FIRM

Laura Chalar

The carpet stretches itself
like a long skin. Under the round

throbbing of a lamp
your hand signs papers

no one will read. Rows of names wait
inside the computers' wombs

while their owners, warm
in their beds, dream contracts.

Outside the frost creeps up; here
a siege of books is thickening,

as ready to defend you
as to never let you go.

The blue wind in the square
will come to erase your eyes

when you leave. For now, you are
guarded by the silent bivouac

of a hundred phones; sleeping
on the other side of air

is the place where your dinner
year after year gets colder.

Those Who Come Our Way

PRO BONO CLIENT

James McKenna

Old, perhaps crazed, but for no reason
kicked out. So I went to court.
The landlord argued only Common Law:

"The old man is a Tenant at Sufferance. Nothing but.
He held only 'naked possession.' No rights at all."
But before I could rise he was on his feet,

voice hoarse: "Your Honor, we are all Tenants
at Sufferance. The house is our body. God
Himself the Landlord." And the judge let him stay.

RUSH TO JUDGMENT

James Clarke

The Hell's Angel with
locks the color of dandelions,
pink muscle T-shirt & gold earrings—a blue
skeleton on a motorcycle, RIDE HARD,
DIE FREE tattooed on his right
bicep—shambled to the witness
box & testified
how he saw the blue Cutlass skid
into the concrete
abutment, stopped his bike &
stayed with the woman whose legs were jammed
under the steering column,
stroking her
hand, whispering to her like a lover &
lost his job as bouncer
at the Brass Rail all-day
strip club for being late.

WINTRY PORTENTS

James Clarke

In chambers this frosty November morning
as I wait nervously, wondering what unsavory
dish the trial coordinator will serve me next:
hit-and-run driver snared in the wheels of
his own cowardice, a couple locked in bare
knuckled combat over custody of an only
child, or perhaps (if I'm lucky) just another
ho-hum specimen of human greed & guile.

I spy the first harbingers of winter parachuting
from the leaden sky outside the window, watch
them hesitate above the asphalt parking lot,
panic in their small, white eyes.

BOOKING

M.C. Bruce

She sat
in the tank
at the booking desk
telling her
stats to
the female bailiff.
A light
shone on
her round
wide-eyed face
and for
a moment she
looked
innocent.

JUDGMENT

M.C. Bruce

Just before the verdict
he climbed onto the rail of the fire escape
on the tenth floor, outside of Department 41,
and jumped.
And even though for a moment
he enjoyed the delicious madness of flight,
gravity's rough embrace
pulled at him
like a judgment.

ABOGADO!

M.C. Bruce

A small round woman clutching
a small round brown baby, another
child clinging to her dress, staring
at me with doe's eyes—the woman
calls me, and the interpreter says,
"She says she's Mrs. Hernandez
and she wants to talk to you."
And I know everything she's going to say before
she says it: My husband didn't
hurt me that badly. We need
his job to keep food in the apartment.
The children are scared, one of them
is sick. The boy had problems at
school. They don't understand why
their father is in jail, and if you
let him out he'll never do this again—
 (I stop her.
I tell her I don't "let" anyone out, I'm
a Public Defender, I represent her
husband and can only try to work
out a good deal for him. She nods.)
"Thank you for
all your help," she says
through the interpreter, with
that submissive manner Mexican women use to
show they understand that the government, whatever
government they happen to be under at the time, is
 going

to do what it damn well wants to do, and they know
that if they piss the government off,
it'll get worse.

I get the guy 30 days, with
good time work time he'll be out
in another week unless INS
gets hold of him.
He looks beaten himself,
in his sagging orange jumpsuit, shriveled and
powerless. I look back
and see her staring,
hope still in her eyes,
at the man who had given her
that bruise on the side of her face.

As I leave the court
I hear her small voice calling,
"Abogado! Abogado!"
running to me with that solemn-eyed
baby still on her hip,
still asking for hope
in a world in which hope
remains in custody.

MIRACLES

M.C. Bruce

He keeps waiting for a miracle, even
though I keep telling him that
the two-year state prison offer
is the best he'll get.
He clutches religious pamphlets
and talks about the Virgin Mary coming
to Vietnam, and that he needs to see the pope
by satellite this August, so that
his sins will all be forgiven
forever.
      Who knows
what heaven wants out of him?
All I can tell him is that the State
of California wants its two years
before they'll even think about
absolution.
      They are jealous of his time,
as if he were being taxed on it.
Just so: It may be easier for him
to get into heaven than
to get out of doing time.

"GOOD MORNING"

M.C. Bruce

I had seen her before on the sidewalks
near the Orange County Jail, her shopping cart
full of plastic bags and secret treasures,
her bulbous coat, her little dirty stocking cap
allowing an underbrush of wild gray hair
to billow around her reddened face.
Today I was walking to OCJ
and she was coming up the sidewalk with her cart,
muttering angry retorts to the air, to herself,
to fate, to someone I didn't see.
And, as I passed her, not looking, walking fast,
she interrupted her diatribe
and said "Good Morning" to me
as cheerful as a schoolgirl.

Confused, I said "Good Morning" back to her,
unsure which of us had been blessed
with a moment of lucidity.

PUBLIC DEFENDER—POEM #34

Richard Bank

Victoria B., who calls me
From the prison and is HIV
And threw hot grease on someone
In an argument in a boarding house
Who now can't be found,
Wants to go home and forget.

Her file is felony green and
New, ready to be handed on
To the next public defender
Who will visit Victoria B.
Again and talk about mental
Health and negotiation and
Confrontation and social
Services and other things
That she doesn't understand.

Victoria B. wants me to be
Her lawyer man, to visit
At the jail and say that
It will all work out,
It will all be fine;
That the terror in the heart
And distended belly with
No one to love inside,
The yellow eyes that show
How far sadness can take
You will go away and

That there will be a place,
A place for you Victoria B.
My pre-trial interview girl,
clinging to hope.

Plead into my voice mail
From the cell block phone,
Play the coquette again
That once you played so well,
Make me use those secrets
That lawyers have, dole out
Like jewels to the chosen few
And set them inexplicably free.

Dream of bail, Victoria B.,
Of your landlady, age seventy-nine
And happy for the rent from your S.S.I.
Push out the dreams where
Demons in the blood take you
Down the path to oblivion.
Despair. Death dreams. Oblivion.

The terror of your unfinished life,
The floating wreckage of all you were—
Adrift, besodden, unmourned;
Swept out of memory, rain
Washing down the angry city streets.
And there is no sign
That happiness is even possible
In such a desperate world.

PUBLIC DEFENDER—POEM #21

Richard Bank

Harold and Jamar, ages ten and twelve,
cut school, walked the west Philly streets
full of sounds and smells and strange
apparitions, crunching delightedly
on the fallen bark of the great Sycamores.

They went happily to see your pit bull pups;
unconcerned, eager for the narrow chance
of a windfall, something to love,
not seeing what almost anyone would know.

You took them to the abandoned house
where you had made a private space;
had a hotplate on bootleg electric,
two mattresses stacked like pancakes and
a kente cloth on the Victorian hardwood floor.

When you had spent yourself, you tied them up
in a delirium and left. They wriggled free,
ran home dirty and hysterical with their tale of terror
spilled out to mothers, grim cops and DAs.

Next to me in a panic in the courtroom
you call them liars. As the two embarrassed
boys pour out their shameful story
despite the stern white judge, I hide
that you refuse to show remorse.
For years you wrote to me from the prison,

drew 666 in the margins, traced your hand
across the yellow foolscap from the law clinic.
The text spoke of Jesus and the Devil. Angels
whispered to you in the hole, wrestled with
Demons for the prize of your immortal soul.
The letters denied each charge meticulously,
point by point, as if it were yesterday.

I never replied, sure that you would forget
us all in time. I keep those letters still,
in the back of an unused file drawer.

PUBLIC DEFENDER—POEM #102

Richard Bank

Kicked out of the house by a restraining order, you lived with friends,
Went to work in a haze, hung out at the bar, disoriented and confused.

In your demented mind, going home drunk at 1:00 AM to get some
        clothes
And talk seemed like a good idea, perhaps sudden forgiveness.

Your half-awake teenage daughter opens the door, sleepy and confused,
Smiles shyly through her braces and says "Hello, daddy."

At this, all of the sadness and terror of the loneliness of the world
Washes over you like a wave sweeping sailors off a ship in high seas.

You push your way in and chase them all out into the neutral night,
Set the couch ablaze and with your hunting bow in hand, prepare for
        martyrdom.

The cops and firemen mill around behind the safety of their trucks, the
        negotiator talks
Through a bullhorn, the neighbors are evacuated in the glare of TV
        lights.

You trade arrows for cigarettes until they are all gone. The entry takes
        you by surprise;
Diversion grenades explode, you flail with a knife, and still, still nobody
        shoots.

Beanbags and pepper spray finally bring you down; they chain you hand
and foot
And haul you off; you shuffle along meekly like a compliant child.

One cop bags his cut radio cord for evidence, the firemen rush in; acrid
smoke,
Hissing steam, and the wail of sirens fade into oblivion as the van drives
off.

Six months later and still in the prison hospital, we discuss a guilty plea.
I describe the lexan SWAT shield arrow-pierced like St. Sebastian.

There are photos of your gutted living room, where once things made
sense.
You nod your expressionless, medicated head and agree.

You will be content with whatever sentence comes, as unafraid
As any other man who has stood at the precipice at the end of love.

PATTERN KILLER ENSNARED

Lee Wm. Atkinson

He sits across the courtroom from me,
slack-jawed, dead-eyed, big hands
bespeak a power otherwise belied.
Plain-faced and non-descript, nothing cries out,
"Warning! Beware!
A killer lurks here, unannounced,
hatred hibernate." His moustache is pallid,
a blond cipher on pale skin, no
statement there, no declaration of his war.

I eye him as a mongoose eyes the snake,
instinctive. Does he know I know?
Does he know the death I would deal him?
The depth of the fear I would share?

A lizard has more warmth, more animated eyes.
My eyes, hawk's eyes, see everything:
the faces of his victims, the cold hunger
of his need. He wakes me:
on moonless nights I start, awake,
feeling the cords of his neck resist my hands.

I shall hear their begging voices in my grave—
I hear them now, pleading for life,
Greek chorused, dead. My justice
little comfort to them now.

ON TEACHING GANG LAW SEMINARS

Katya Giritsky

we only talk about trying
to clean up the messes left behind
when children too young to drive
spend their after school hours
shooting at each other
with real guns

we never talk
about how young they look
sitting in court
skin still baby fine and tight
under the shaved hair
under the tattoos
under the shackles

UNDERFOOT

Ann Tweedy

at one point along the river,
the grass was so lush i was afraid
to step there, as if some living, breathing
thing hidden underneath
caused that springiness, but i stepped
and stepped again, marveling.

not far from Eugene, Oregon, can i say this?
an unmarried middle-aged man made himself
a friend to the neighborhood. he restored
cars on property he rented and hired
out-of-work fathers to help him. summer
nights, on couches and car furniture
outside his trailer, joints passed freely.
hot days, he lined a truck bed with plastic
to make a pool for children to play in. little

by little, girls and boys loved him. one laughing
six-year-old slid naked on a bedspread only to imagine
its pompoms as the frills of his mustache.
she said she played with him repeatedly alone
in his trailer, while, just outside, her mother
watched her older brother. a four-year-old
taking a bath explained how he licked
her pee pee as mommy raced home
to record the lion king. at trial,
defense counsel tried to confine the girls' families
to the chalk marks of alcohol, pot, and poverty.

THE MADMEN AND THE LAW

John Crouch

The madmen and madwomen pound every morning
On my email box, and show me the wounds
The law has ripped in them and their families.

After ten years of this, I sit down with my father,
A veteran of the last revolution—
Defender of Abbie Hoffman, freespeakers,
Druggies and conscientious objectors,
Indians with imprecise objectives,
Victims of police brutality,
Prosecutorial witchhunts,
And child abuse hysteria,
Of innocent parents whose kids were taken
And molested in backwoods foster-homes—
And I ask for advice on my own revolution,
Which he believes in, sometimes, more than I.

"The first people you get to fight the oppression,"
He explains, "are always so warped by it
They can't function, damn near sink their own cases,
But you start with them, if you start at all."

No Singing in the Courtroom

ELEVENTH FLOOR LIES

Warren Wolfson

This is a place
where minor matters are decided.
Here, on the eleventh floor of the courthouse,
I conduct a reluctant venue
for lawyers. Only small injustices occur.

I demand explanations. Tardiness is unacceptable.
The lawyers tell me lies about
where they were and when they left. No one,
certainly not I, believes the lies.
If they were dropped on a scale
they would barely press.

Still, I accept the lies. We must
get on with it. Cases are called
and I decide them. Someone wins
and someone loses. The number of people
in the courtroom remains the same,
but the faces change.

The lies are lost, replaced by other lies.
We pretend and we proceed. People leave
with more or less of something.
Decisions require words. At times
I look up from papers, to the wall.
On the wall I see: In God We Trust.

MISPLACED BLAME

Warren Wolfson

> A power failure blamed on a cat shut
> down the Cook County Criminal Courts
> building Monday . . .
>
> —*Chicago Daily Law Bulletin*, 9/26/03

Let's not blame the cat.
He, if he was a he,
had a right to find
a warm, safe place
to rest until dark.

The cat did not know
the white powder was dropped
at the detective's feet,
or placed for finding
on the car's cold bright leather seat.

The cat did not see
what the worried witness saw—
the hooded man running
after firing the bullet
that ended an unfulfilled life.

The cat did not commit
the stickups or burglaries
or aggravated sexual assaults
or any of the other ways
men and women find to offend.

The courts closed for a day.

No trial, no prison term,
no decision to kill a killer—
a restful 24 hours.
Then it all starts again.

HOLY THURSDAY

James Clarke

In the Egypt of Landlord and Tenant court
at Brampton this Holy Thursday,
where a throng from
all races, creeds, and walks of life
murmurs in the rotunda:
tenants who can't pay rent,
landlords who can't pay mortgages,
unemployed fathers,
single welfare moms,
the mentally afflicted,
the physically disabled,
scoundrels, saints, everyone

lugging a sack of bad luck:
no money, no job, Powers of Sale, leaky
roofs, faulty furnaces, flooded basements,
dripping faucets, attic squirrels,
sudden sickness, government treachery,
hungry children,
runaway husbands,

there are no tambourines
of thanksgiving,
just the rough deliverance
of the law,
with no paschal blood
on the door posts
to guide my slippery sword.

THE JURY RETURNS

M.C. Bruce

They slowly feel their way into the box
As if blinded by what they know they've done.
Not looking at us, file one by one
With passive faces, sad and blank as clocks.
My client's hands are folded tight, shaking.
He searches every eye, then knows he's trapped.
He sees the verdict on their faces, mapped,
And hears the cell door shut. As if waking
From justice's slumber, the Judge now stirs
To ask the clerk to read the fatal note,
The jury form, which seems to slowly float
Into her hands. But then the crash occurs:
"Guilty." "And this is what you each do say?"
Each nods "yes"; all then quickly look away.

JUVENILE DAY

Charles Reynard

Like loaves and fishes, a miracle
to find one desultory day each week
amid traffic days, motions days,

felony days, here in Heart Break:
courtroom on the second floor,
the intersection of South Surrender

and West Submission, where
I sit and await with mumbled prayers,
the coming of those like Danny.

The law, in its due and majestic process,
assigns fault, sometimes responsibility.
There's a difference, I frequently say

from my benchtop Olympus, incanting
the fifteen-minute legal liturgy, called
Permanency Review, once every six months.

Wherefore, I find it is not your fault,
Danny, that you have Post Traumatic
Stress Disorder, Oppositional Defiant

Disorder, and RO BiPolar illness.
Or that you are under the influence
of Depakote 500 mg, Zoloft 200 mg,
and Seroquel 40 mg. But it is

your responsibility not to swallow
shampoo or thumbtacks, not to run

away, steal gas, shoplift matches
from Dollar General, and not to knife
your neighbor or your nurse during

the manic phase of your moon,
the unspeakable sorrow hidden
behind your chaotic chronicle

(which we cannot talk about because
you may break, Family Service says,
even though you are doing better).

Blessed, son, I hold you in my hand,
so helpless to help, so blind to watch
over you in your garden of griefs.

CONSPIRACY OF RIVERS

Charles Reynard

So natural that all of them
would swear the oath, pour their
conflicting stories into turbulent,
muddy water roiled from conjoining
testimonies, like a conspiracy of rivers.
It is the burden of truth to suffer
its abrasions, beveled by rules,
filtered with objections,
before it is welcomed as proof.
The relation of truth and proof
is not often any more
than a ragged slant rhyme.
Court is an alternate universe:
search for truth and *due process*
chance cousins of arcane
genetic origins. Cynical good fortune
if they were to meet in the corridor.
Truth is the gift wrapped in the elegant
cloth of doubt (called *reasonable*),
ribboned in systematic rubric,
finally named justice.

THE MAN CHILD

Barbara B. Rollins

I am the judge. He is the man-child, just past the watershed
seventeenth birthday. Before three other judges he is an
adult, charged with adult misdemeanors. In my court he is
a child charged with murder because nine months ago he
followed the home boys.
He followed the home boys and drank beer.
He followed the home boys and drank gin.
He followed the home boys and took Valium.
He followed the home boys and smoked weed.
There was a peckerwood, a white man who presumed to invade
        the sanctum of the Hood.
The wood was a loser.
The wood was an old man at 38.
The wood was HIV positive.
The wood was drunk.
The wood was contentious.
The wood was in the wrong place.
The wood singled out the lady sitting on a car and demanded a light.
The wood and the lady argued.
The lady was friendly.
The lady had been friendly with the old home boy.
The lady had been friendly with the young home boys.
The lady had been friendly with the man-child.
The old home boy socked the wood for the name of the lady
    and the Hood.
The wood lay on the pavement.
The young home boys hit the wood with quart beer bottles.
The young home boys hit the wood with gallon gin bottles.

The man-child hit the wood and he hit him and he hit him.

The heat came. Everybody left. The wood lay dying on the pavement.

I am the judge of the man-child.

I am not the judge of the man-child's mother who let him grow
up a wild child and would not come to get him when called.

I am not the judge of the man-child's father who disappeared
after the genesis and does not know the man-child. It is said the
man-child's father now lives with the man-child's step-sister as her
man.

I am not the judge of the man-child's step-father whose leaving
prompted the man-child to transform from a good student to a
Crip home boy in two brief years.

I cannot judge the juvenile system that kept slapping his hand
and sending him home to mama, when she would take him,
and to his aunts and grandmother when mama would not take
him.

I am the judge of the man-child. God help me, I am the judge of
the man-child.

A LATE AFTERNOON BREACH
IN THEIR RANKS

Bruce Laxalt

Six in the dock, murder-one on the marquee,
Late-summer show time at the county courthouse.
Six of the defense bar's court-appointed finest their champions
Deployed at counsel table before them like stalwarts.
They, the scruffy as-yet innocents, sit shoulder-to-shoulder behind,
Their squinting eyes suspicious with wonder at the oaken pomp,
The twitchy glare of the deputy like an electric fence around them.

Middle-age white-trash drug deal gone bad,
But now the hair's been trimmed, slick-plastered back
From the pasty foreheads of six faces rode hard.
The cheap suits new, ill-fitting, sinews and callouses
        emerging from the cuffs,
Sprout wrinkled necks and darting eyes from their collars.
Though if truth be told, scant difference at first glance
        between first and second phalanx,
Except the suits at counsel table are tailored,
And not all the eyes are alcoholic.

A clever opening gambit, the collective century's street wisdom:
First to rise for the admittedly mangy but unjustly accused,
The five-year rookie, earnest dew still on his face,
The fiery innocence in his eyes fixed dead-on in accusation
Of the three-piece-suited sophistry of the prosecutor's opening.
A fine young man, the matronly jurors nod sagely among themselves.
Surely he would not deceive us, nor defend a guilty man—
Though, if truth be told again, several eyes cannot but wander
        to the nether row.

And later, unexpected luck:
The D.A.'s second witness, temporarily saved by subpoena
    from deportation south,
Just i.d.'d the wrong blond-white-guy as the one with the gun.
Quiet chuckles at counsel table, muted catcalls and toothless grins
    from behind.

Three-thirty recess while the judge grabs a smoke.
The illusion of ranks dissolves with the bang of the gavel.
The lawyers mill, trade jokes, crude quips
    about the now-wounded prosecutor
    now bent pompously over his notes as if in secret study,
Check their watches for the approaching cocktail hour,
And roll their eyes in mock exasperation to their civil litigation cohorts
    in the gallery
Stopped by for a few minutes comic diversion and feigned
    nostalgia.

The clients, momentarily off-stage, now ankle-manacled
    to their chairs,
Have scooted closer for a quiet and hurried confab.
Except one, skinny guy, second from the right, whose lawyer,
Older guy there, now joking with rest,
Just dropped the jury a hint he might jump ship.
He looks quickly out of the corner of his eye
At the manically whispering backs of his former friends,
Then stares instead at the ceiling,
Feeling suddenly, in the hot and rancorous din
    of the late-afternoon courtroom,
As cold and alone as he's ever been.

OFFERINGS TO AN ULCERATED GOD

Martín Espada

—Chelsea, Massachusetts

"Mrs. López refuses to pay rent,
and we want her out,"
the landlord's lawyer said,
tugging at his law school ring.
The judge called for an interpreter,
but all the interpreters were gone,
trafficking in Spanish
at the criminal session
on the second floor.
A volunteer stood up in the gallery.
Mrs. López showed the interpreter
a poker hand of snapshots:
the rat curled in a glue trap
next to the refrigerator,
the water frozen in the toilet,
a door without a doorknob.
(No rent for this. I know the law
and I want to speak,
she whispered to the interpreter.)
"Tell her she has to pay
and she has ten days to get out,"
the judge commanded, rose
so the rest of the courtroom rose
and left the bench. Suddenly
the courtroom clattered
with the end of business:

the clerk of the court
gathered her files
and the bailiff went to lunch.
Mrs. López stood before the bench,
still holding up her fan of snapshots
like an offering this ulcerated god
refused to taste,
while the interpreter
felt the burning
bubble in his throat
as he slowly turned to face her.

TIRES STACKED IN THE HALLWAYS OF CIVILIZATION

Martín Espada

—Chelsea, Massachusetts

"Yes, Your Honor, there are rodents,"
said the landlord to the judge,
"but I let the tenant
have a cat. Besides,
he stacks his tires
in the hallway."

The tenant confessed
in stuttering English:
"Yes, Your Honor,
I am from El Salvador,
and I put my tires
in the hallway."

The judge puffed up
his robes
like a black bird
shaking off rain:
"Tires out of the hallway!
You don't live in a jungle
anymore. This is a civilized country."

So the defendant was ordered
to remove his tires
from the hallways of civilization,
and allowed to keep the cat.

SING IN THE VOICE OF A GOD EVEN ATHEISTS CAN HEAR

Martín Espada

> —for Demetria Martinez
> Albuquerque, New Mexico
> August, 1988

The prosecutor spoke "conspiracy"
as if Demetria were a mercenary
trading in helicopter gunships,
not the poet with a reporter's notebook.
The prosecutor spoke "smuggling"
as if two pregnant refugees
were bundles of heroin,
not fleeing a war of slit bellies.
The prosecutor spoke "illegal aliens"
as if El Salvador were a planet
of brown creatures with antennae,
not mestiza women dividing in birth.
The prosecutor spoke of conspiracy
to smuggle illegal aliens,
indicting the poet with a poem,
her poem for two women of El Salvador,
traveling with them by way of Juárez,
evidence abducted from her desk.

So Demetria, accused, stood in the meandering
patient line of all the accused:
accused of ducking searchlights and gunshots
on the border, crossing the river
to steal televisions from sleeping suburban dens;

accused of mopping in slow lazy rings
or letting meat burn in the spitting grease;
accused of bruising the fruit with bruised hands
picking for so many nickels paid on the bucket;
accused of the bristling knives and needles,
the slash and puncture of the tattooed arm;
accused of leering with an accent
at the cheerleaders of private high schools;
accused of causing ear infections
by jabbering *en español* at the bar,
or pangs in the teeth of those
who mispronounce their names;
accused of skin so brown their brains must shrink
with every promiscuous generation;
accused of kissing the welfare check twice a month
so the man with a pickup truck paying taxes
can never buy a boat;
accused of conquering territory in potter's field,
crowding cemeteries with crosses
like commuters on the subway at rush hour.

But the dead, those dead exhausted
by the drumroll of accusation,
heard the indictment of Demetria.
They knew she walked at the elbow of pariahs,
quietly singing sanctuary. So the dead opened their mouths
and began to sing, not the soprano of choirs glowing white,
but the rough-throated song of people at work
or pausing from work in barrios and fields:
the heart-attack seamstress, the lettuce-picker in pesticide fog,
the boy who painted murals before the bullet.
In México, her peasant ancestors

sang the *corrido* of Demetria the Renegade to Zapata's troops.
In El Salvador, the dead with amputated tongues
could suddenly sing, their music floating like steam.
Together they would sing in the voice of a god
even atheists can hear, even a jury across the border.

And the poet was free.

THE OLD JUDGE

Steven M. Richman

We are conversing in the soft tones
reserved for such occasions, wine
freely flowing, a few vodkas, but
mainly a discreet crowd, pillars
of the legal community, keepers
of the holy order of things.

The old judge enters, liver-spotted,
bent, hands shaking, eyes rheumy,
born the day the last German left the trenches
in the war to end all wars, to land himself
behind German lines in the next war
to end all wars, Bronze Star, Silver Star,
Purple Heart—all the colors of bravery,
for justifiably killing men.

He is small at the head of the table
as we gaze with fixed smiles,
an assemblage of respect and awe
and wait for him to speak, to impart
what we presume he must have,
after all these years, after all that service,
after deciding right and wrong,
all those cases, those complex disputes
that only people can make for themselves.

He looks over the last of our heads
as if searching for a window in the blank wall:

"They were all guilty," he says, as if himself
on trial, before a judge we cannot see.
"All guilty," he repeats, and smiles,
lifting his wineglass and studying
the deep purple glinting
in the flickering candles, and says
nothing more.

MONDAY MORNING BLUES

James Clarke

Entering the courthouse out of the bright
epiphany of morning sunlight

you leaf through the file on your desk & as is
your custom review

the salient facts of the young offender you're
about to sentence.

Before the courtroom door groans open
you steel yourself one last time

before the bathroom mirror, bury your
qualms deep inside the thick

court file and stride into court hoping no one
will hear your pulse racing

beneath your smooth silk robe, feel the blue
torque of the law

clamping round your heart.

A CERTAIN IMAGE

James Clarke

haunted the judge's dreams.
Standing over a deep well
he grips the ankles of the guilty
and before he lets go
glimpses terror
on their faces.
Then, pity ticking in his ear,
he leans his head
into the rounded darkness,
waiting
for the splash.

WHITE FEATHER

James Clarke

During morning break
    his deputy came to him
in Chambers
    holding a long
white feather.
    "I found it in the
courtroom," she said,
    astonished,
as though evidence
    of a bird on the wing
had no place
    in the halls of Justice.
"I wonder where it came from."

BURIED IN THE SNOW

James Clarke

How odd I know
to overhear oneself say
at 3 o'clock
on a winter's day:

"We want the truth,
the whole truth &
nothing but the truth,"
a blizzard blowing
cold blue needles
outside the courtroom window.

THERE ARE COURTROOMS

James Clarke

with dusky
   windows,

parodies of
   Holy Writ,

where plush
   arguments

rise like
   colored

balloons &
   blow away,

apathy finer
   than talc

sifts down the
   the long

afternoons in
   waning light,

dusts the
   immaculate

cuffs of counsel,
   the eye

of justice grey.

SINGING IN THE COURTROOM

M.C. Bruce

There was singing in the courtroom
a light, rambling
rhythmless child's tune
hummed loudly by the boy
in the back. The judge
stumbled on the plea,
pausing before sending
some guy to the pen
for nine years. The bailiff
rushed back,
the handcuffs clinking on
his belt like a tambourine.
The lawyers and the guys in the
cage all looked back as the
boy skipped away from his
mother, singing even when
the fat bailiff shushed him and
frowned. He was not impressed
with the tedious majesty of the law.
Finally, his mother
caught him in her arms, and whispered
to him and took him
from the room. And the courtroom
heaved a sigh and went back
to the business of putting men
in prison.
  Later in the hall
I heard him again, and said

"You can't have fun in here,
it's not allowed." But he smiled
at me, like he knew
I was joking and
I wished I was.

What Logic There Is

CONSTITUTIONALS

David Leightty

Strict Constructionalist

This man of letters holds, deep-delved in books,
His purpose firm, his quest the law that's there;
Bound by the page's height and breadth, he looks
And finds it plain, direct, precise—and bare.

Situationalist

Confidence lies in his certitude.
Vaulting from page to clause construed.

Interpretations

Meanings arise here like the green of trees—
Staying, then scattered with the Sibyl's leaves.
Still bearing this rank season's tangling yield,
The trunk stands rooted in a tangled field.

ECONOMICS FOR JUDGES

Charles Reynard

> "Give me a onearmed economist!"
> —Harry S. Truman

When they spoke of predators, prisoners
(and their dilemmas), free riders, yellow
dogs, toxins, adverse selections, moral

hazards, it sounded like our candyass
normative values disintegrating
on sharp stone shoals of unforgiving facts,

like kindergarteners caught in a Freddy
Krueger film. All that we needed to do:
find the one-armed economist somewhere

between *ad coelum et ad infernos*,
to drive us in his special purpose vehicle,
fueled by CAT bonds, out of the nightmare

on Wall Street to the efficient frontier
where we learn minimum wages did not mean
to cause joblessness, nor was it intended

that increased fuel economy causes death,
nor did deregulation ever marry greed.
We hope at last it's there, where we

find equilibrium, the point of no regrets
where we dig up the black box
for judging, found with this recipe:

Put in the facts, add a notion or two
of law, shake well, the answer tumbles out.
On the other hand, if the box is not found,

we will exist here, consoled by a new way
of *economic thinking* (remember *thinking
like a lawyer*, the ornament of argument,

wretched proofs of our lawschooled gift?),
knowing that the cost of living has not
yet diminished its popularity.

LONG ARM

Charles Reynard

One wonders about the law, its
mysterious anatomy,

whether its long arm warmly drapes,
like it was mother's arm reaching

across the daughter's bent shoulder
to console for oppressing grief.

The disciplined among us, those
whose knuckled vocabularies

have been rapped most effectively
by our nuns and Jesuits, say

(and sound like we finally know)
it is about jurisdiction

of the person, about such things
as rendition, warrants, summons,

cerebral replicas of words
once thought (mistakenly) to be

in English. One wonders whether
she has more than one, as in her

loving arms, and whether the long
one is hidden while the short one

tires, holding up scales, or whether
the other arm was severed clean

in the first personal injury
accident before banner ads

on buses and television
(no fee until [not unless] you win).

DRAWING LINES

James Clarke

Find a footloose fact,
adhere to the multiplication school
of fish times fish
whose shadows silver
beneath your pen.

A flight of thought is seldom
straight, so never forget
you are the Law, revising
a flat & improbable world,
picking the straw
from your neighbor's eye.

CAUGHT IN THE NET

James Clarke

Only three days into this trial
and already I'm in a sweat,

for it's becoming apparent that the
Plaintiff, a small fish in a big sea,

will be swallowed up, bones and all,
by the Leviathan Trust Company

whom he dared to bite. As judge
I cling to the raft

of impartiality, hoping for a miracle
—that the Plaintiff, like Jonah, will

escape unscathed but, alas, it is not to be.
My plea to settle is rejected and God,

it appears, is in no mood for miracles.
The case rolls on like a tidal wave

as the net closes and I resign myself
to my role

as eviscerating shark of justice.

SUN SHOWER

James Clarke

I slouch out of the cold, hard mouth
of the Courthouse where lawyers make
a feast of trouble, lost for the moment
in the ambivalence of judging others,
the pulley of the law still creaking in
my ears, half nodding, half forgetting
who I am,

to be startled awake by a cool breeze
whipping across my face, raindrops
flicking off my bare skin & high above,
wildly winging over the trees, a scraggle
of crows scrolling out my name.

TOWARD A DEFINITION OF LAW

James Clarke

Law dresses in black silks, wears a coat
of thick paint, curls her hair with a cork-
screw, never powders her face in public.

Law seldom writes in straight lines, loves
the fripperies of words, hums in riddles &
slant rhymes, commonly finishes a sentence

with "without prejudice" or "on the other
hand." The eyes of law glow like radium;
her laughter, the sound of delirium.

Law rarely blushes, never says she's sorry,
shuns looking in the mirror, steers clear of
dark stairwells and long, unlighted corridors.

■

Simon Perchik

As petitioner
he cues the Act of Bankruptcy
whereby, wherein and wheretofore
all his debts dissolve
on that blue litmus
of hocus pocus
every debtor waves
to disappear in front of creditors.

Collected now
all debts are filed with the filing fee
gone and he goes
counting the house.

IN CHAMBERS

Richard Krech

"It's the most high stakes poker game
in the world," he said,
exaggerating only slightly,
leaning over in his chair towards mine
as we spoke in quiet voices
heard by no one else in the chamber.

Advocates and adversaries
sitting in a circle
as they have for years.
The black robe in the center
of attention, the center of power,
the robe changing its inhabitant
on a cyclical basis.

Showing enough of your hand
to create a threat to the opponent.
Keeping as much powder and ammunition
dry as possible
for use in battle if it comes.

Presenting technical legal issues
or broad constitutional claims
always against a factual background
limited by provable facts
and evidentiary objections of your opponents.

Always the facts. Yr skill
or that of the adversary
must always bow to the provable facts.

Yet the sieve of evidentiary objections
of "hearsay" and 352 and 1101(b),
the sieve of "judicial discretion"
strains that factual material
so thin sometimes,
so fat at others,
that its rough weave
resembles the truth
like a general outline
but details, perhaps crucial
perhaps not, are distorted.

SUMMARY JUDGMENT

Paul Homer

The Lepidopterist peers with cool delight
into each cage where his nocturnal catch
of moths swarm about a light,
mirroring in their panicked aimless motions
the transience of facts and our emotions.
A Luna, trailing behind her long ethereal
green gown, is encircled by the arrogant
royal purple of a lordly Imperial.
Alone in his cage, a nocturnal one-eyed giant,
the Polymorphous, clings,
red hate in eyespots on its wings.
A wrinkled Cecropia, an outstretched velvet glove,
    floats above
a tipsy, white, and madly dancing Gypsy.
Now he takes one from its cage,
stills its final fluttering with some
cotton in a jar, and primly pins it to a page
with nothing yet written thereon. It lies inert,
unchangeable, beneath the eyepiece of his inspection,
judging head, thorax, abdomen: each complex section.
All facts are pinned down now without dispute.
All further inferences are rendered moot.
He writes his final measurements upon the page
without a moments hesitation.
Nor will the Judge who hears our years of petty litigation
grant any plea for further time or for amendment,
    or delay one day his
Summary Judgment.

THE LEASE

Paul Homer

—on delivering the Women's Library Club
lease to Writers Theatre

Like an organism that in a frenzy feeds upon itself
and needs no food from fridge or shelf
but multiplies by parthenogenesis,
a Collective Memo menaces
the sickly phrase, the legal blunder,
tearing each asunder
as it uncoils along its paginated way.

One can only stop this fearful feeding
by a document which on close reading
is impregnable, filled with so many definitions,
counter-admonitions, charming circumlocutions
requiring locks upon the washroom, keys for every door,
until, as a famous fighter prayed,
"Please, *no mas*, no more."

For here, dear counterpart,
is the product of our mutual art
for signature.
A lease that may endure
in the history of war
with Thermopylae, with Ilium and Troy
acclaiming the heroic feats
of Halberstam and Homer,
of Nagelberg and Adams,
of Jim and Peg Malloy.

DRAFT OF LEASE

Paul Homer

> —written to opposing counsel, whose client,
> a theater group, insisted on terms for a lease
> of performance space that differed from a prior
> letter of intent

Three years the writers worked upon the script
with collaborative invention, finally content
that what it said
expressed their clear intention.

What the writers failed to see
after public hosannas, is that after
Acts One and Two
someone else would write Act Three.

A new producer skimmed through each page
and announced "this thing won't play on stage.
For a start let's change these parts, omit
these troublesome lines.
It's what we call in architecture
a total redesign."

But one writers' group objected to
this different manuscript,
saying perhaps the curtain should come down
before it's gone up,
unless this new producer
sticks to the agreed script.

LAWYER DOG

Kenneth King

You would think a lawyer wouldn't have to worry

About being sued, but I guess if you hang around people who

Hang around courtrooms, you should maybe expect them to go

Crazy sometimes, like you're the gun they tried to shoot somebody with

And they missed by god and so the damn gun must not be shooting
    straight,

So throw the damn thing on the floor. I mean if you see a whining,
    snarling dog

Being set on by a pack of coyotes and you stick your hand in there
    thinking

You're going to help the dog (for a small fee, of course) you shouldn't be

Surprised when it turns around and bites you. You're just one more
    thing

To gnaw on. Of course some people think lawyers are the snarling dogs
    in the first place,

And if you're the dog going woof-woof by god why did you look
    cross-eyed at my master you

Shouldn't be surprised if some scruffier dog comes along and says woof-
    woof why did you screw up

My master's life. I mean a dog is a dog is a dog and a dog has to bark at
    somebody, and if there ain't

Anything else on the street then you go barking at other dogs. Not
    just barking either but rushing in and

Biting the sons of bitches good, I mean we're talking a death hold if
    necessary, we don't want

Master thinking we're not on his case or he might sue us. And admit it,
    by god, you screw things up

All the time, you catch the judge in a bad mood and you just happen to have the wrong look in your eyes that day,

Like if the judge kicked you, you might snap back or something, which is
exactly the wrong look to ever have

Before a judge, because the judge is the judge is the judge, and the judge
does whatever the hell the judge wants to,

Short of shooting you, or taking bribes in open court, and that's the dirty
little secret we don't

Tell our clients about, really, most of the time, like

It doesn't really matter what the law says, if the judge really wants to go
a certain way he'll find

A way to do it, and the only thing to keep a judge half-honest is the other
judges, which is a bit

Like lawyers guarding lawyers, or auditors auditing auditors, woof-woof
you big bad crooked lawyer dog,

I'm going to sue your sorry ass, which is one hell of a note. So if I sue a
doctor and I screw up,

My client gets another dog and he sues me, and then I got to get

A dog of my own, and then maybe the insurance company doesn't want
to pay, and so I get

A dog to sue them, and maybe he screws up, and I get a dog to sue him,
and it's hard

To sleep in the middle of the racket. I mean, we got a serious dog problem
here and I don't know

What to do about it, my malpractice is $1000 a year, and that's without
the extended tail, meaning

If they sue me after I get disgusted and quit, the insurance company ain't
going to pay,

Because the tail costs extra. A dog without a tail is just walking around
daring some other dog

To sic him. So I got to find that many more people to bite just to pay my
premiums

So if I don't bite somebody just right they don't send in

146

Some hungrier dog to take me on. I mean if this keeps up
I'll be suing myself, biting my tail and gnawing my legs off.

AFTER MEMO-WRITING

Greg McBride

—after Frost

Like the apple picker crumpled
on his cot sleep-counting russets
by the thousand falling round
his head, falling, tree to bucket rim,
then rumbling to the cellar bin,
my sleep is troubled by memoranda
spilling from fluorescent years,
their half-remembered lines
from not so long ago, as I
consider my career, when I
had a thing or two to say
that seemed to matter, prose that lay
in laser-scribed perfection
on the page, words as bound to one
another as the ladder rounds
that rose together, one then one,
toward the clarity found in late
autumnal sky. It was the art
of memoranda, persuasive
as the fecund apple tree, one hoped,
though sometimes tossed aside as little
more than litter, like bruised russets
to the applecider heap;
and then, especially, when wanting
only sleep, I'd feel the tendons
of my writing wrist worn sore,
the way the picker's instep arch
would ache. It's late, and yet, I cannot

help but marvel that it was the prose
that bought this kitchen table,
this paring knife, this place, in which
I slice an apple fallen from
the apple picker's sleep, and, sleepless,
taste the loss of memo-writing time.

AN OFFICE WITH A VIEW

Greg McBride

Nothing prepared me for life in the sky,
in this narrowed concrete pencil which spires
toward a clouded underside. Yellow cabs
lurch and buck on the child-sized street below.
Across a lake of thinned air, a fellow
crossword tower blinks randomly awake.
A muted morning light has gathered
and settled, slatted across the hard-to-match,
three-cushion sofa, which loafs, off-blue, between
these standard lamps, inscrutable beneath
their burned-out bulbs. Perhaps they'd shed some light
on the truth of matters here. I'll have to ask
Diane to tend to that. The teal and mottled
carpet sends up scampered motes, like fairy dust
that might transform a life or, perhaps,
the in-box memoranda here for me to sign,
in vain if yesterday is any guide.
And these journals piling higher on the corner
of the desk nag like questions unaddressed.
The sun burns through the mist and ravages
the carpet fibers, one by one. Teal flashes
gold then blue. The plain's afire. I ride
my father's shoulders, July 4th, beneath
the sudden conflagration and thrill to lean,
to touch the sky, above, below, the luxury
of this spot in space wholly unforeseen.

THE ESTABLISHMENT MAN

Bruce Laxalt

Yes, I am, indeed, a lawyer still,
Near twenty five years, and yes, still
Stolidly keeping the barbarian trumpets at bay
From the fragile walls of Jericho.
My rounds are watchful, so others may have the peace of sleep,
My path a crumbling step away from gravity's sweet call,
But staked out nightly like a child's garden path
And my dogged struggle for law and order.

At first, clear eyes on the path of right,
Young enforcer, stern voice for the ancient rules.
A simple task, and simple truths:
For peace disturbed or stolen,
Repayment in the coin of time.
From righteous law, sweet order will surely follow,
Like dawn the cruel chaos of night.

Later on, the civil courts—less simple now.
White shirts and starch, greying hair and tired eyes,
I rise respectfully amid oak walls,
The company's bulwark against the plaintiff vandals.
Decorous tones and the sweet light of reason
Coaxing, gathering the frightened horses
To the center of the jury box,
To the fleeting haven of peace and order.

And now, near fifty, and late at night,
Childlike, I putter and fret over the meal's remains,

Wash and scrub, and scrub again the glasses and plates.
Table, and table again.
There is indeed both law and order here,
Dirt and shameful grime wiped clean, or neatly concealed,
Searching always for the last hidden shards and tiny crystals
Of hurled fury and smashed decanters,
Careful always that the dumb stare of dawn
Shall see nothing amiss or out of place.

My plaintiff friends across the courtroom aisle
Make joyful chaos with their craft,
Throw the world with glee against the jury-box wall
And wait with sheepish grins to see the morning's designs.
My career has been otherwise.
I do my dishes,
And determinedly set about my task
Of tidying up.

BOILERPLATE

John Charles Kleefeld

This agreement dated the ___ day of ___
by and between ___ and ___
(jointly, We and Us).

Know all persons by these presents:
Time, we agree, is of the essence.
We're much obliged.

Our heirs and successors
administrators and executors
and permitted assigns—jointly and severally,
    we bind (perhaps to their surprise).

Whereas, hereinafter,
heretofore, whereafter.
Whatever.

Do this, promise that,
quid pro quo, tit for tat.
Good and valuable consideration
    (the receipt and sufficiency of which is hereby acknowledged).

This is our entire Agreement: no warranties, guarantees, sureties
    or security,
except as in Schedule A. It's not a question of misanthropy,
just certainty, finality.

Notice by mail and/or facsimile transmission;
a contract's no place for preterition,
Let's cover all our bases.

Disagreements? Mediation, arbitration,
some provision to avoid litigation,
but just in case—invalidity of any part of this Agreement
  shall not affect validity of the whole.

Choice of laws and choice of forum
damages clause, fixed or *ad valorem*,
We're almost there now.

Execution's alright in counterpart,
residing as we do miles apart
yet—*ad idem.*

Lo! A work of beauty, our joint travail,
this Agreement, ironclad, none can assail,
until we part.

See you in court: ___ *v.* ___.

TWO EPIGRAMS

David Leightty

Explanation

to a spouse—how a lawyer
has made so little money

The hardluck cases came to me, afraid;
Seldom the fortunate in shining hour.
Thus was I blessed to lift the weak, unpaid,
Unburdened with the gain of wealth or power.

Attorneys General

on Veterans' Day

"Suicide mission!"
　　　　　　　　But the gripe was false—
Just lawyers with a loser case to try.
The risk? Nothing but money—the client's loss.
No matter what, no one was going to die.

THE PRISONERS OF SAINT LAWRENCE

Martín Espada

—Riverview Correctional Facility
Ogdensburg, New York, 1993

Snow astonishing their hammered faces,
the prisoners of Saint Lawrence, island men,
remember in Spanish the island places.

The Saint Lawrence River churns white into Canada, races
past barbed walls. Immigrants from a dark sea find oceanic
snow astonishing. Their hammered faces

harden in city jails and courthouses, indigent cases
telling translators, public defenders, what they
remember in Spanish. The island places,

banana leaf and nervous chickens, graces
gone in this amnesia of snow, stinging cocaine
snow, astonishing their hammered faces.

There is snow in the silence of the visiting rooms, spaces
like snow in the paper of their poems and letters, that
remember in Spanish the island places.

So the law speaks of cocaine, grams and traces,
as the prisoners of Saint Lawrence, island men,
snow astonishing their hammered faces,
remember in Spanish the island places.

IN THE HOUSE OF THE LAW

Betsy McKenzie

Now, I have made for myself
A small mouse's nest
Beneath a cornice
In the grand house of the Law.
Comfortably curving
Walls that hold
The trembling soul
Like a bird held
In a gentle hand.

THIS IS IT

Michael Blumenthal

—for John McNally

Ah, John, the world is cold
and we are in it. But
there is a place of no ice,
and sometimes I wake, look
through the windows of all my neighbors,
and they are rising from their beds
and drinking their coffee, and they
are leaving their houses to catch a bus
that will take them somewhere they have
no use for. But John, this is the world:
the street, the bus, the garbage,
and all the imperfect lovers who are
willing to love us despite our imperfections.
Not the heaven we dreamt of, but
the sweet sewage of something better
and worse that flows in the streets
and we have no choice but to call: home.
This is it. And if we say it, again
and again, we may yet believe it:
This is it. This is it. This is it.
The fragile envelope we call body,
the huge ambivalence of love, and the
dust we clean from our shelves and will
eventually turn to. *This is it,* friend:
the oak and the empty cup; the starling
and the half-burnt candle; the women
we are always leaving, and the wise women
who leave us before we turn to them in anger.

Let's say it again: *This is it.* This is
the white sky of November and the bird shit
that plops on our shoulders without warning
or reverence. This is the rain
and the old garments we have no use for,
the cruelty and wild wonder of not knowing
what we want. *This is it,* friend,
this is it. On this incalculable Thursday.
On the day of your birth. Happy Birthday.
This is it.

The Ravages of the Work

ESCAPE

Joyce Meyers

All I remember of my escape
is the leather briefcase, wine-colored,
smooth, that grew from my hand.
It replaced my face, a curtain
across the pain, a shield
against emptiness.

I carried it everywhere, stuffed full
of tools and disguises, tomahawks,
feathers, old maps, new machines.
In time it grew heavy, my shoulders
sagged. In the dark,
when no one was watching,
I let go.

Without my ballast, I float
in mist and fog. My feet strain
for the solidity of earth, wet soil
between my toes, stone surfaces
glinting in the sun, a path
through dense woods
redolent of wild mushrooms
after rain.

IN THE CLUTCH

Kathleen Winter

As my Wills and Trusts professor said,
When you carry a hammer,
everything looks like a nail.
When your hammer is poetry,
everything's a poem,
even the horrible pet-store rabbit
loosed on Sonoma Mountain,
furtive but bright white, elliptical,
low to the ground, scuttering—
not exactly greased lightning
on those rabbit's foot feet—
across the road at dawn.
Last week, my husband spotted it
against the autumn weeds.
How that rabbit survives
from one day to the next
is mystery to me,
and how it came to be here
and what furred or feathery inevitable
will snatch it up
to feel the shudder of its misplaced life.

SAFARI

Steven M. Richman

They hack their way through the jungle
with silk ties. Gentle swishing sounds
mingle with bird calls.
Younger hands haul laptops filled
with necessary court opinions.
Calls from unseen animals make them pause,
cocking their head in readiness.
The courtroom fills with exotic
beasts drinking from the cool waters.
Suddenly enters the litigator.
Trust and estate lawyers flee with gazelle-like hops.
Corporate lawyers freeze.
Sauber is on one in a flash,
briefs and pleadings around the throat,
the jugular neatly slit, gushing blood.
After several seconds of silence, the others
resume, warily, their refreshment.
The sounds of the jungle return.
They only eat, after all, what they kill.

LETTERS OF CREDIT

Steven M. Richman

He looks deeply into the mirror of his children
but cannot see himself, though he knows he is there,
somewhere in the depths. They speak to him
with the greatest politeness, and if there is affection
he feels it as the slightest warm breeze in summer,
a hot dying breath of presence, not of comfort.

He works their love like his job, studying precedent
and applying law to fact, to derive a holding, a balance
of truth, justice and equity, completely anomalous
in the calculus of emotion. Still there is a sense of obligation,
like throwing coins into the tollbooth—regardless of whether
they hit, or bounce off the rim and roll away, the debt is paid.

They are gone, glimpsed through materializing letters
on the instant messaging boards of computer screens,
or in the electronic conversions of voices to ear, heard
like the ocean in shell: false, imitative, distant and faint,
or like letters of credit, carrying his value into the void
of commerce, of life, to distant lands he will never see.

THE TEMPTATION OF SAINT ANTHONY

Steven M. Richman

No one will eat with him this night.
Just as well. Too much law. He is spent.

In L'Amadeus on Rue van Reynn, once the
Brussels studio where Rodin sculpted,

Sauber orders fish stew,
heavily creamed, and Chimay beer,

brewed by the monks as devotion
to God. The thought amuses,

and he compares the fermented deal
he closed earlier to such divinity.

That night he dreams of the
Temptation of Saint Anthony,

but it is he who sits in the midst
of the Bosch nightmare, no Dali

simplicity to cloak the demons
that vanish upon waking.

WAX

Nancy A. Henry

After the hearing
After sifting the detritus of violence and dysfunction
I am in my car
I turn on the radio
I take off my shoes
I roll the windows open to everything
Which is unlike that which dominated my morning.
My heart is hungry for the world
Beyond this little community playhouse of pathos
Where we act out monotonously sad
Yet hideously various dramas
"In re: Girl X," "In re: Boy X,"
In all their sorry splendor and array.
I am not complaining.
I have chosen this domain
The public dumpster of the judicial system,
Other people's mess,
Which seems to stick to me on days like these,
Makes me want to turn myself inside out
And stand out in the rain.

These afternoons I wax the floor.

How can I explain the mystical healing effect
Of this practice somehow restorative of faith and sanity
Conjuring the essence of all that is good, dignified and noble
The purifying herbal smell of carnauba wax and lemon oil
Transporting me

To small New England libraries with dark wood shelves
Worn leather chairs, old books with covers like saddlery,
The smell of deep and holy quiet.
To graceful echoing churches
Where I have seen worn arthritic women run soft rags
Over altar and pew, floor and rail
In the attitude of reverent pilgrims
Praying Stations of the Cross,
Wisps of white hair straggling from under kerchiefs,
Clumsily hidden halos.

There are people who do not scream,
Who do not spit and accuse,
Lie and scratch and burn and tear at the
Tender flesh of babies,
Fail to feed them, break their bones
Sell their small doomed bodies for drugs
Slake with them their rage and fevered hungers.

I will summon them now,
The people who write the books,
Those fine aged works
Of noble sensibility
Of great and ordered thought.
Those strong and humble women who caress the smooth wood,
Light the candles,
Who turn for one last look
Cross themselves, touching knee to floor,
Though no one is there to see.
I run these thoughts around in my mind like a cool white pebble.
I close my eyes and breathe in the knowledge
Of heroism and selflessness in people.

I believe in the Communion of Saints.

I will sit like this for a long time,
Rubbing the long oak boards
Till they softly shine
Till they glow like blessed candles
In the empty church.
In an hour my own children will come
Down from the school bus steps
Across the sweet green lawn
My own children safe and well
My own children fed and whole
And we will embrace,
And we will embrace.

BABY'S FIRST BATH

Nancy A. Henry

The dead infant
is scalded white and scarlet
a horrible piebald fish.

Beside me at counsel table,
the gentle social worker who found him,
the cop on the stand
who took the picture,
breaking down.

Do you need a moment, officer?
No, I'll go on. I can go on.

No inept parent's failure caused this
though I'm sure the careful warnings
were a helpful guide
to what was done so awfully well.

There is enough ugliness you will live to see
without my putting this dead baby
in your head.

Forgive me.
He cried so much in my sleep
I thought he needed more people
to hear him.

OUR FORTIETH YEAR

Nancy A. Henry

—for Kelly

We were two lonely women
Taking autopsies to bed
Rising at four
To prepare our cross-examinations
Remember how we avoided dreaming
Remember how we awakened screaming
We had our hot dogs at Simones
We had the cops we fantasized about
The work that kept us sex-horrified
And sex-deprived
We had our court officer with his gun
We had the narrow filthy bathroom
Across from Courtroom One
We had our antidepressants
Our Ambien, our tallboys
And our scotch
We had our divorces
We had no time for therapy
We had our nervous breakdowns
One by one
We both swore we were right
We both prayed we weren't wrong
We both feared our witnesses lied
We each did our best for either side
We brought home stray dogs
We rarely dared to pray
We never, ever cried.

WIDOW'S WEEDS

Bruce Laxalt

Home late again from the office, I fear—caught up again
In medical reports, or dog-eared childhood books,
Or other tomes on mortal man. Still, there is another hour
Of sunlight left us below the eastern Sierra foothills,
Before the shadows from the tallest peaks engulf.

Your car, its engine already cooled, sits in the driveway
Locked. No waiting dogs in the courtyard for me tonight,
I hear faint barks from far away. The house late-summer quiet
And warm, your grocery sacks on the counter, my briefcase is
Suddenly out of place on the front-hall floor.

Coat and tie discarded to a dining-room chair,
I walk in silence to the back-yard deck.
There far off across our grass and pines are you,
The dogs chasing each other in the distance,
As you bend, weed, water, and tend your garden flowers.

Already a widow, I've left you such,
Strong and alone on a solitary summer evening.
I stand unnoticed on the deck and watch,
And hesitate to hail from afar, to disturb,
To announce my already dwindling presence.

WORK IN PROGRESS

Bruce Laxalt

There you sit, lost among the trophies on the office shelves,
In the dusty detritus of a quarter century's thrusts and parries,
More of interest to clients now than me.
There in the back, you are a shy one—a 5x7 photo, peeking out.
Ignored, it seems, by the nightly cleaning staff,
Untended, the dust grown highest and unkempt around you.
Slowly lost, over the years, in the cluttered and momentary
    exhibitionism
Of last month's trials and verdicts.

"What's that?" an occasional more curious visitor will exclaim.
"Many years ago," I reply, "a work in progress."
"A beauty," they'll say. And indeed it is.
Red orb suspended in the black of space, a delicate planet.
The rivers, in deeper tint, wend their elegant way through the
    highlands,
This way and that, in graceful contretemps,
To the planet's edge and beyond, to the velvet black of void.
"That's the back of a child's eyeball," I add. "In hemorrhage."

A work in progress, indeed it is, sweet child.
As were you, at three.
Eager eyes and sun-tinged hair, a soap-sudded grin from the
    porcelain tub,
The only photo we could find to show the jury
Of the work of art you were, and would have become.

The neighbors heard your nightly screams, muffled
  By the apartment wall.
  They never called in.
Your case worker broke down on the stand.
  Did you know you'd been on the schedule
  for a next-week's visit?
Your bartender mother's boyfriend, his own sweet scared eyes
    open wide
In silent supplication to the jury, begged for merciful belief:

"She fell in the tub."
I and the jury thought not.
The doctors said you might as well have hit concrete
    in a three-story fall,
And showed the jury the photo of your bleeding retina—
Sad beauty—staring blindly out of the glossy color print,
Caught unawares in the private act of dying.

And now, near fifty, and late at night,
Childlike, I putter and fret over the meal's remains,
Wash and scrub, and scrub again the glasses and plates.
Table, and table again.
There is indeed both law and order here,
Dirt and shameful grime wiped clean, or neatly concealed,
Searching always for the last hidden shards and tiny crystals
Of hurled fury and smashed decanters,
Careful always that the dumb stare of dawn
Shall see nothing amiss or out of place.

THE GAME CHANGED

Lawrence Joseph

The phantasmic imperium is set in a chronic
state of hypnotic fixity. I have absolutely
no idea what the fuck you're talking about
was his reply, and he wasn't laughing,
either, one of the most repellent human beings
I've ever known, his presence a gross and slippery
lie, a piece of chemically pure evil. A lawyer—
although the type's not exclusive to lawyers.
A lot of different minds touch, and have touched,
the blood money in the dummy account
in an offshore bank, washed clean, free to be
transferred into a hedge fund or a foreign
brokerage account, at least half a trillion
ending up in the United States, with more to come.
I believe I told you I'm a lawyer. Which has had
little or no effect on a certain respect
I have for occurrences that suggest laws
of necessity. I too am thinking of it
as a journey—the journey with conversations
otherwise known as the *Divina Commedia*
is how Osip Mandelstam characterized Dante's poem.
Lebanon? I hear the Maronite Patriarch
dares the Syrians to kill him, no word
from my grandfather's side of the family
in the Shouf. "There are circles here"—
to quote the professor of international
relations and anthropology—"Vietnam, Lebanon,
and Iraq . . . Hanoi, Beirut, and Baghdad."

The beggar in Rome is the beggar in Istanbul,
the blind beggar is playing saxophone,
his legs covered with a zebra-striped blanket,
the woman beside him holding an aluminum cup,
beside them, out of a shopping bag, the eyes
of a small, sick dog. I'm no pseudo-aesthete.
It's a physical thing. An enthusiasm,
a transport. The melancholy is ancient.
The intent is to make a large, serious
portrait of my time. The sun on the market
near Bowling Green, something red, something
purple, bunches of roses and lilacs. A local
issue for those of us in the neighborhood.
Not to know what it is you're breathing
in a week when Black Hawk helicopters resume
patrolling the harbor. Two young men
blow themselves up attaching explosives
on the back of a cat. An insurgency:
commandos are employed, capital is manipulated
to secure the oil of the Asian Republics.
I was walking in the Forties when I saw it—
a billboard with a background of brilliant
blue sky, with writing on it in soft-edged,
irregularly spaced, airy-white letters
already drifting off into the air, as if they'd
been skywritten—"The World Really Does
Revolve Around You." The taxi driver rushes
to reach his family before the camp is closed—
"There is no way I will leave, there is no way—
they will have to kill us, and, even if
they kill every one of us, we won't leave." Sweat
dripping from her brow, she picks up the shattered,

charred bones. She works for the Commission
on Missing Persons. "First they kill them,"
she says, "then they burn them, then they cover them
with dead babies . . . ." Neither impenetrable opacity
nor absolute transparency. I know what I'm after.
The entire poem is finished in my head. No,
I mean the entire poem. The color, the graphic
parts, the placement of solid bodies in space,
gradations of light and dark, the arrangements
of pictorial elements on a single plane
without a loss of depth . . . . This habit of wishing—
as if one's mother and father lay in one's heart,
and wished as they had always wished—that voice,
one of the great voices, worth listening to.
A continuity in which everything is transition.
To repeat it because it's worth repeating. Immanence—
an immanence and a happiness. Yes, exquisite—
an exquisite dream. The mind on fire
possessed by what is desired—the game changed.

IN THE HOUSE OF LAW

Charles Reynard

Sent at an early age to live in the house of law,
    he sat alone in the dining room at the veritable,
steeped in a glazed pot of verity, no room for rest.
    The practice, rhetoric's dance on heads of pins,
found no truth, though for sake of contention,
    he argued its presence as guest.

Rooms in the house of law bawled with phones.
    The kitchen tossed salads of convoluted fact
with abandon, dressed in preternatural cunning.
    No living rooms, dreaming rooms, only rooms
with Daumier prints, for waiting, for worry.

Would she claim this wreck of law,
    disguised as man in disarray?
Fevered overdue process corduroyed his brow
    shadowed in the venue of alone.

Could she shred his contract, consume his tort,
    strictly deconstruct his holy constitution,
charm his statutes? Might her patience sit
    astride his trembling body of years,
braid, from ribbons of all his brilliant briefs,
    a valedictory of his longings?

One last hope-filled offer: to be her door
    in this house of law, to be a density
for her to open, walk into his emptiness,

spacious space, anomaly of soul.
Come again, he asked, with hinges and oil,
    with deadbolts to secure me as I close
behind you, clothe you with the nascent night.

SHOW TIME

James Clarke

On the marquee today,
a new drama.
Observe the lawyers
in their natural habitat:

that is to say,
on display. Regard
their furtive stalking style
crouching behind words.
The dark intent beneath the smile.

Speared by the judge's piercing eyes.
Polite assassins. Under contract.

RESPITE

James Clarke

The judge was too old & wise to
believe everyone would follow

the little legal verities that wobbled
off his tongue; sometimes fleeing

the courthouse, sunk so low by
the drip-feed of constant lies he'd

listened to all day—not even a
reasonable facsimile of "the truth,

the whole truth & nothing but the
truth," he'd rush home to climb into

bed, wait impatiently for sleep to
drift up like a little boat with its

cargo of dreams to bear him away,
knowing through it all that the respite

would be fleeting; come daylight &
the return of the unadorned truth of

living, his old worn toothbrush would
still be there to bring him back to earth.

IN THE EASY DREAM

Susan Holahan

you're standing in the Court, all nine Supremes
in your face, before you notice your nightgown
flapping at your ankles when you stamp
a bare foot on the Fourth Amendment (Searches
and Seizures) point. It's the flannel one your
mother sent two marriages back: small purple
and orange flowers; high neck. Decent if
you keep it buttoned. Not what you mean to
argue in. Wrist elastic rides up if
you wave your arm. You tend to wave your arm.

Simple, they say: *You're not ready for this.*
You don't say when you work at home like this
you turn into Wonder Counselor, the only
presto-litigator who can hold the line.
They'll overturn us back to coat hangers.

In the other dream that hangs on like shame
from the time you waltzed in front of strangers
oblivious while blood spread across the back
of your pearl-gray skirt, the love of your life
turns away from you a face you never see
at meals or on the pillow when he's asleep
and you're still reading: a face hard as death.
Whatever you have on, you can't give him
an argument—you, all words. Every time,
you wake weeping. *Simpleton.* You're not ready.

LETTER OF RESIGNATION

Federal Trade Commission, Bureau of Competition,
Washington, D.C., 1974

You've heard of people calling in sick . You may have called in sick a few times yourself.
But have you ever thought about calling in well? It'd go like this: You'd get the boss on the
line and say, "Listen, I've been sick ever since I started working here, but today I'm well
and I won't be in anymore."

Call in well . . .

—Tom Robbins, *Even Cowgirls Get the Blues*

Dear Boss:

Some mornings on the way to work I stare into my rearview mirror and the
world cries out like an abandoned lover whose only wrong has been fidelity.
The tulips along the hillside seem mute and eloquent like the prayers of
an autistic child, and the shared ambition of the chickadees seems the best
success any man could hope for.

Take the Cherry Blossoms, for example, working their way to a brief
fruition like an old poet and dying as if in shock when anybody takes the
time to notice. Strange, boss, how the times we're really in the world we
call tourist, how the brief attention we give to anything beyond ourselves
passes laziness.

Nights alone now, I listen to the gossip of earthworms and trust the quiet
the way old fishermen trust the wisdom of patience or the justice of a
barren line. I work hard at my laziness, and the best work I do no one will
ever pay for. Some day, though, I'll turn this little car around, call the breath
of azaleas bottom-line to my accounting. Don't worry about me when that
happens, boss. Just call it a private success . . . . Call it my own promotion.

Sincerely

Michael Blumenthal

THE METAMORPHOSIS

Michael Blumenthal

It is just as you feared
it would be:

Your life has gone on
without you in it—
weather and happiness are still indifferent
to anything you ask of them, your friends
say they have missed you, but refuse
to stop sleeping with their wives, pleading
the approach of November, dreams of serpents.
Loneliness, which knows no season, hovers
over everything like a detective.

You wake in the same bed
you have always dreamt of filling
with something larger than yourself.
Mold has settled in the coffee pot like
sadness, but defers to you,
comes clean. The post office had talked
of changing the zip codes, but has done nothing.
All the other travelers can reach you now,
can send you pictures of your small self
smiling before the Palace of Athena, of
old Greek fishermen beating your tentacled body
against the stones, making the scaly flesh

soft, devoid of breath,
easily chewable.

FORMER ATTORNEY OFFERS PRAYER OF THANKSGIVING FOR HIS NEW JOB

Michael Sowder

—for Ford Swetnam

I thank you, God, for this poem today, whether or not it'll be
   any good,
and for a new home in a town called Preston with a desk under
   a window of sky and the cries of cranes,
for a full moon that rises over the Bear Mountains at twilight
   and falls past mountains at dawn,
for a river named Bear that tumbles out of a canyon, meanders
   by our house, with hot springs, kingfishers, osprey, and trout,
for our neighbor, Ezekiel, who comes to the door with
   cucumbers and carrots for the forgiveness of sins and
   hopes for our redemption,
for new words, like *jack-Mormon*—reminding that even in
   Zion apostates like dandelions grow,
and *gravity water* which runs down hills, which the city doesn't
charge for, which rises over fields in silver jets, swords
crossed against the desert sun,
      for my commute across the bed of an ancient sea that one day,
      14,000 years ago, broke its dam and spilled north for hundreds of miles,
for the oranges and reds of autumn spilling down watersheds
   of Oxford, Bonneville, and Scout,
and the aspens that etch the fir-dark peaks in gold,
for light dawning clear as the Mediterranean,
while magpies rise from the nameless dead of the road where
   they dine in tuxedos—Republican cousins of the crows,
and for my arrival in Pocatello, where treeless hills fold over
   each other with a Renaissance love of the naked body,
   a U.P. town of rails, cowboys and poets who, it has been said,

actually—and I shit you not—like each other,
and for a boss who says, *Write poems, not briefs.*

For this is a beginning, and it's good to be beginning,
as Whitman and Merton and St. John of the Cross said,
for we'll always be beginners any day we're alive.

And now the streams are tumbling with syllables,
and the sea's rhythms are printed on the land,
cranes trace calligraphs across the evening sky,
and rocks break like words on the ground.

IN ANSWER TO THE STUDENT WHO ASKED IF I STILL PRACTICE LAW, AND WHY NOT

Lee Warner Brooks

For this one sonnet, I have paid, in foregone
salary, approximately two
hundred and fifty thousand dollars, on
conservative assumptions. They accrue
in my imagination, wealth compounded
on a daily basis—what was called,
in law school, "time value of money"—rounded
to the nearest clotted vein or bald,
embattled skull. I wonder who, perceiving
what the future holds, would budge one finger
toward it? Or would even grudge the leaving
of it? If the pay had made me linger
there, I'd never have had cause to rhyme.

Lawyers Do Grow Old

THE LAWYERS

Barbara B. Rollins

They arise as the judge comes back into the court,
two on opposite sides of the bar.
They have stood here before and in other courtrooms—
over forty years' practice of law.

On the left is the hero of injured and maimed,
the old personal injury don
with his silvery mane and his homely demeanor
concealing words crafty and wise.

To the right the defense is insurance in shoes,
though he sits with the woman who drove.
While his hair still is brown, he is parting it now
just an inch or so over his ear.

In their sixty-fifth year the attorneys at law
butt their horns, and for what? Not for much.
The request isn't quite up to forty-two grand
Though the fervor and feeling are high.

But the game is the same and it's deep in their bones
so they'll fight 'til the contest is done.
For the goal is as much the defeat of the foe
as a verdict declaring it won.

TESTATION

Richard Bank

> "He was an old-fashioned judge.
> The kind lawyers try to avoid."
> —obituary

Snaking down the faux Medici steps
and around the cluttered city block,
clusters of prosecutors and pols
are waiting patiently to show their faces.
The deferential cops and all the suits
speak the power now gone for good.

I am among the onlookers: the heathen, the estranged.
I, who had been called in from the hallway
to start again, unable to console the terrified,
who waited their turns like lambs
and watched the imperious fury,
the eager delight at sentencing,
the harsh reality of his tumultuous trials.

We hated to work his room;
the sham *voir dire*, the frenetic process,
technical and full of minutia and dread.
Now, with the surprised widow
and the respectful old men filing by,
there is an air of triumph to it all,
the spectacle a vindication in itself.

Then some of us took note of happenstance,
finished up our business there
and joined together for dinner and some wine,

taking delight in the change of pace.
The living spoke with the living
and we left the dead alone.

END OF AN ERA

Richard Bank

Publisher Commerce Clearing House
Sold to Dutch concern for 1.9 billion.
—newspaper headline

I remember you in the solemn stacks, oh CCH;
wrestled with your cold vinyl bindings
when I was the angel-headed hipster
abandoning beatitude for love and war
with an agonizing slowness.

Soon you will be gone to the low country
where the ganja still is best, they say,
this side of Kathmandu, Kabul, Cali
or even Chester County gold
in what seems like just a breath of time ago.

The ones who refused induction
changed to witnesses with hapless tales
and I, who was the longhair then,
now attend reunions well spoken, grave and thin,
"my collar mounting firmly to the chin."

Tourists walk the market at Pleiku.
The old bones groan and settle, empty.
How much the path we take depends
on who we are and not the race we ran.
The child is truly father to the man.

A STATUTORILY PROTECTED CLASS

Paul Homer

I am a member of a statutorily protected class,
which I'm quite glad to be
if only by reason of my longevity.
I'm proud to be companionate
to horned owls and chickadees,
speckled finch and purple slate.
Each month I wait for my AARP edition
to determine my position on affairs of state:
prevention of threats against erosion
of my Social Security,
vacation of that witless law
that taxes my estate,
articles on how much can be paid
to children to qualify for Medicaid,
a new and innovative statutory assumption
which I'm advised will aid
in preventing job dismissal regardless of merit
thus avoiding the indignity of grin and bear it,
or how the absence of a marital deduction
may not lead to a net worth reduction
or any need to share it,
as a member of a statutorily protected class.

AMONG THE PERENNIALS

Jesse Mountjoy

Each time I water the hostas, the astilbes, the ferns,
I think of the old lawyers of the past,
Like Davis Williams of Hart County,
Who carried a fresh cut onion half tucked
In a pocket of his waistcoat, for tears for the juries,
Or Uncle Harry Ward of Bourbon County,
Thumping his long hickory cane on the courtroom
Floor for each point of law or equity,
Or my cousin the judge, with a voice like a cello,
Or smiling, blind Ed Prichard, with his single, stiff nods
Behind leaded glass as he fondles law books
Like a spinster browsing through love letters.
My dreams are compost heaps of passionless meditations.
In my garden, in the sacramental, elusive hours,
With my elders, I can engage in Victorian studies
Of phenomes and the luxury of damnation.
The fragrance of illusion is everywhere.
The summer rounds its curve, and then I dream
Of poet lawyers, home from work, my age now.
For example, Wallace Stevens, still vested
After a day at Hartford's insurance offices, walking
Among the shade perennials, endlessly repeating
The word "subrogation"
Under the toneless air of his plants.
Among my shade perennials the hose's spray drums
Their leaves with sounds that resolve my dreams
On one day and give them a longer life
On the next, and with whispers that all that is
Imaginable of this world is necessary to it.

APOSTROPHE

Howard Gofreed

O Goddess of Opportunity!
You called to me unexpectedly
years ago in a Maryland bank lobby.
My hand had the stairwell door
to return from an escrow deposit
when I heard "Howard" shouted
with female joy. Turned round
overwhelmed by the tousle of blond
California hair, warmth of tanned
California torso, invite of wide
California hips half hidden inside
sunny shorts, amber arms and bold
California legs placed just so
one before the other, yellow cotton
halter blouse tied loosely between
California breasts above which
nestled a captivating come
hither California smile. I
did not recognize you from high school.
You seemed to have emerged newborn
and dry from the Pacific, raising
unpeaceful passions in me. I,
dressed as a three-piece lawyer,
was not prepared, reacted
like a cartoon character: smoke
whistled from my nose and ears,
a fire alarm clanged in my head,
my tongue came out, grew

in amazement, as did my popped
eyes. I flashed through hot colors
to red, sizzled to ash before you.
Your smile broadened slightly
and nestled more deeply in your breasts.
I remember saying you looked great
and wanting to drop the deposit slip,
forget that old farmer upstairs,
my client, awestruck by shelves of
leatherbound law, wanting to run off
with you anywhere, somewhere,
nowhere, to a room without windows,
without a door, but alas!
the inertia of marriage and job. We
settled for histories: you back
visiting from California, me hiding
the left hand.

Now you return to me—
divorced from the wife
and the law, bifocaled, teeth
crowned, paunchy and balding—
in dream. O Goddess of Lost
Opportunity, we run off!
and I wake shaking, haunted
by where in my head
you have hidden so long.

WORK

Lee Robinson

The girl who knelt in that suburban sea of grass, the girl
who combed St. Augustine for weeds, a penny apiece,
what did she learn? That the hues of green are as many
as the million grassy fingers tickling her palm,
that it takes a hundred weeds to make a dollar.

The girl who worked at the branch library, the girl
who shelved books at the library all summer
after seventh grade, what did she learn? That books
are very heavy, even the slim ones. They smell of sex
and death. That there is never enough time to read.

The sophomore who served breakfast in the college
dining hall, who stood like a good soldier before the field
of bacon and eggs, what did she learn? That six
in the morning comes too soon and disappears always
too soon, that the faces of strangers are full of grace.

The senior in the nighttime cleaning crew at the Farmers'
and Merchants' National Bank, Boston, 1969, punching
the clock in her blue uniform, what did she learn?
That the restrooms of men are messier than the restrooms
of women, that wastebaskets overflow with secrets.

The graduate teaching English in the middle school,
whose grammar screeched like a frightened animal
pinned against the blackboard, the graduate at 21 before
her class of 35, what lessons did she learn? That nothing

is black and white, that Black and White is everything.

The lawyer just out of law school, tending to the indigent,
the indicted, the threetime housebreaker, the ungrand larcener,
to the man who denies he put his cock inside his daughter,
what did she learn? That guilt is what we breathe, as plentiful
as air. That innocence is rare and far more frightening.

The lawyer in her middle age, in her little cage of suit
and stockings, her arms filled with the files of the deserted,
the divorcing, the unsupported and the unsupporting,
what did she learn? That no story is the same as any other,
that love is ever ingenious, always uniquely disappointing.

And the woman who sits at the kitchen window, the woman
who is finished with offices, who sits at the table, whose
window is the world and whose work is this poem, what
does she know? That this is her fortune—this poem, made
word by word, beginning with the girl who kneels in the grass,
beginning with the girl on her knees in the grass.

CURRICULUM VITAE

Lawrence Joseph

I might have been born in Beirut,
not Detroit, with my right name.
Grandpa taught me to love to eat.
I am not Orthodox, or Sunni,
Shiite, or Druse. Baptized
in the one true Church, I too
was weaned on Saint Augustine.
Eisenhower never dreamed I wore
corrective shoes. Ford Motor Co.
never cared I'd never forgive
Highland Park, River Rouge, Hamtramck.
I memorized the Baltimore Catechism.
I collected holy cards, prayed
to a litany of saints to intercede
on behalf of my father who slept
through the sermon at 7 o'clock Mass.
He worked two jobs, believed
himself a failure. My brother
believed himself, my sister denied.
In the fifth grade Sister Victorine,
astonished, listened to me recite
from the Book of Jeremiah.
My voice changed, I wanted women.
The Jesuit whose yellow fingers
cracked with the stink of Camels
promised me eternal punishment.
How strange I was, with impure thoughts,
brown skin, obsessions,

You could tell by the way I walked
I possessed a lot of soul,
you could tell by the way I talked
I didn't know when to stop.
After I witnessed stabbings
outside the gym, after the game,
I witnessed fire in the streets.
My head set on fire in Cambridge,
England, in the Whim Café.
After I applied Substance and Procedure
and Statements of Facts,
my head was heavy, was earth.
Now years have passed since I came
to the city of great fame.
The same sun glows gray on two new rivers.
Tears I want do not come.
I remain many different people
whose families populate half Detroit;
I hate the racket of the machines,
the oven's heat, curse
bossmen behind their backs.
I hear the inmates' collective murmur
in the jail on Beaubien Street.
I hear myself say, "What explains
the Bank of Lebanon's liquidity?"
Think, "I too will declare
a doctrine upon whom the loss
of language must fall regardless
whether Wallace Stevens
understood senior indebtedness
in Greenwich Village in 1906."
One woman hears me in my sleep

plead the confusions of my dream.
I frequent the Café Dante, earn
my memories, repay my moods.
I am as good as my heart.
I am as good as the unemployed
who wait in long lines for money.

THE MAN WHO NEEDED NO ONE

Michael Blumenthal

He wanted to need no one, not
love or thirst, not even sunrise
and the sweet amulets of water
that fall from the heavens.

No, he wanted to be an island
of self-sufficiency, to sleep
with his arms around the pillow,
a jack-in-the-pulpit alone on his throne
in the damp woods, singing to himself
beneath his curled umbrella.

And this is how he lived for many years—
a solitary song, a soliloquy
spoken into the small mirror
that hung above the wash basin,
with its blue towel and basket of dead flowers.

But something remained wrong—
a dull ache whispered from below his voice
where his heart should have been, a seed
rumbled in the pit of his stomach as if to suggest
a tree that had never grown, a stone skimming
the surface of water once and then sinking.

He grew old this way, never knowing
it had been need he had needed all along—
the sound of his own small voice

asking for a light to see by, a match
to retrieve his heart with from the widening dark.

MEMORIES

James Clarke

haunted the old judge, rolled around
his head like polished pebbles: the look

of her hippie leather sunhat as she
stooped to pick daisies on a sunlit hill,

her limbs a clear calligraphy against
a milk blue sky, the tears that ran

down her cheeks that morning in the
open field when she told him all was

forgiven, that she was ready to try
again. No inkling then with death so

far away, of all the might-have-beens,
the small, cold betrayals that lay ahead

between first light and the slow return
of evening—the long & slippery

footbridge of love.

AT THIS POINT

Warren Wolfson

The first years
were tilted, angular, passionate,
at times adversarial, like a trial,
punctuated with tenderness
and recesses of tacit forgiveness.

Then came the comfort times, featuring
soundless speaking, like early Chaplin,
the passion still there,
but breathing easier,
separate peace declared.

Now we have reached
a resting place,
a promontory,
looking east,
to the precious days.

Going Home

LAMENT

Paul Homer

I lack the wit and dash of Ogden Nash
Those hints of Browning's ducal crimes
That hide within his rhymes,
Walt Whitman's unrepentant storms
Rejecting our accepted norms;
Langston's darker notes and hues:
A saxophonist riffing blues,
Sandburg's urban elegiac,
Biblical, chanted, quite Hebraic.
No—not for me the great ones' foyer—
That's why I became a lawyer.

NIGHT MOTH

James Clarke

Between stars and screen
the moth
with iridescent body
and seven white notches
on delta wings,
       listens
to the cantillations
of the frogs,
prisoner like me,
caught in the shadows.

LEARNING BY DOING

Michael Blumenthal

And now the day is mine and it is sweet,
I take this message from the light and make it real:
The loss we do not claim we must repeat.

Who knows if it is possible to cheat our fate?
In our denials, our wanting we reveal,
And the day is sometimes lost, and not so sweet.

A man can get through life—it's no great feat
To walk along the earth, or else to kneel.
But the loss he doesn't claim he must repeat.

Who lives alone, another doesn't cheat—
To wake alone at night and not to feel;
To call the day your own and make it sweet.

I've nothing more than words to seal my fate.
There's little that I want, still less I need.
So the loss I do not name I must repeat.

Who doesn't hate the unrelenting seed?
Who doesn't think his life's often unreal?
This day could be yours too, and could be sweet.
Just claim your loss tonight. And don't repeat.

LIFE ON APPEAL

Richard Krech

One heartbeat at a time
we keep going forward
towards our ultimate verdict.

Live yr. life the best you can.
There is little likelihood
of success on appeal.

GOING HOME

James Clarke

Be patient.
We are going home.
It is not far. We are rocking
in the great belly of the ship.
No light cracks the dark sea, but
the ship is strong, the voyage
will not be long.

We will arrive early.
It will be morning. We will
rub our unshelled eyes, see
the shore rise.
We will untangle our bones & play
in the lemon groves, dwell
in a white house near blue water.
There will be time. Be patient.
We are going home.

Compilation of the Anthology

James R. Elkins

One might imagine an anthology of poetry that focuses on love, death, children and marriage, on birds and flowers, rivers and mountains. But what can be said of an anthology devoted to the poetry of lawyers, that focuses on the legal world and on the work that lawyers carry on in this world?

We are not likely, today, to think of lawyers as the kind of people we associate with poetry. We assume that lawyers are hard-edged, aggressive, argumentative, rational to a fault, and predisposed to rhetorical practices that would leave them unlikely to be found as poets. We imagine poets differently, if we can imagine them at all. Tim Nolan, in his introduction to the anthology, calls attention to the fact that our stereotypes of *poet* and *lawyer* are diametrical opposites. The idea that a lawyer might be a poet, and a poet might practice law, jars our sensibilities, and unsettles what we think we know about lawyers and about poets.

I am a lawyer. More accurately, I am a lawyer who ended up teaching law. I know these stereotypes first-hand. When lawyer poets first appeared on my intellectual map, I viewed them as something akin to exotic birds who had lost their migratory bearings. Following Tim Nolan's astute observations on poet and lawyer stereotypes, I can confirm that these stereotypes tell us something, just enough that we allow them to overstay their unannounced arrival and infect us with the false sense that we know more about how the world of lawyers and the world of poetry works than we actually do .

Over the years, I have focused my teaching on law and its place in the tradition and practices of the literary and liberal arts. Working on one of my courses—Lawyers and Literature—I discovered the fiction of a writer named John William Corrington. Corrington, I learned, was a novelist and English professor, a screenwriter and student of philosophy, who took up the study of law at age 40, and began to make law and lawyers a part of his fiction. But the thing about Corrington—who was largely unknown in legal circles—I found most intriguing was that *he was a poet when he became a lawyer.* Whenever I sat down to write about Corrington and his lawyer fiction, I found I was forever puzzling over this curious fact: *Corrington was a poet and a lawyer.* Obviously, I suffered from the stereotypes that Nolan describes.

When I chanced upon Corrington's fiction, I knew exactly two lawyer poets: Archibald MacLeish and Wallace Stevens. I knew about Archibald MacLeish because he had written about his dual citizenship in the worlds of law and poetry in the *Harvard Law Review.* Wallace Stevens, as is widely-known, was an insurance company executive who became one of our most widely known modern poets. What is sometimes forgotten is that Stevens was trained as a lawyer, worked his way up through insurance company ranks as a lawyer, and identified himself throughout his career as a lawyer, not as an insurance company executive.

Curious about lawyer poets, I asked my friend, Lowell Komie, a Chicago lawyer and writer whose short stories I have taught over many years, if he knew of any such exotic creatures. Komie reminded me that Edgar Lee Masters of *Spoon River Anthology* fame was a Chicago lawyer, and that Charles Reznikoff had a background in law. With my less-than-grand list of five lawyer poets, I suspected there must be others. Marlyn Robinson, a reference librarian at the University of Texas's Law Library, quickly rounded up a list of twenty or so lawyer poets for me, and it began to dawn on me: *I had had a glimpse of the surface of something that runs deep.* I began to search out old poetry anthologies and what I found—the pages sometimes crumbling in my hands as I turned from poet to poet, poem to poem—stunned me: many of our early poets were lawyers. They were not, in the first century of this country's existence, rare and exotic creatures at all. Our early lawyers were also our poets. I spent a summer creating a website to recognize the lawyer poets I once thought of as exotic. I called the website "Strangers to Us All: Lawyers and Poets."

In that first summer, when I set out to identify lawyer poets, all

I wanted to do was write a few pages about the puzzling fact that John William Corrington was a poet who, at mid-life, decided to become a lawyer. But to write those few pages, I ended up reading about Archibald MacLeish and his agonizing decision to abandon the practice of law to become a poet, to move his family to Paris and become a literary man. I learned that Wallace Stevens practiced law and composed poems all of his adult life and saw absolutely nothing unusual in being a lawyer and a poet. Surprisingly, I found that Stevens, MacLeish, and Corrington had virtually nothing to say in their poetry about being a lawyer. With Edgar Lee Masters and Charles Reznikoff, the situation was a bit different: Masters did not shy away from presenting lawyers and judges in his poem epithets. Reznikoff made his name as a poet by distilling old judicial opinions into verse. In a summer's work identifying America's lawyer poets, I found I had tapped deep into an historical substrata and an exemplar of the continuing place of lawyers in the liberal arts tradition: From the days when the first lawyers arrived as colonists to take up residence in the "new country," legal advocates took up their business in a new land and—in surprisingly large numbers—became our earliest novelists, journalists, historians, travel writers, and poets. History pulled the rug from beneath the convenient labels of my stereotypes.

When I began my work on lawyer poets and their place in history, my interest in poetry, was negligible. It never occurred to me that identifying lawyer poets would require me to read poetry. I was not a poet, had little experience reading poetry, and, consequently, had little interest in the contemporary lawyer poets turning up in my Google searches. I had no idea why a person might want to read poetry or why I should want to read it. Yes, I would identify myself as a *reader*, but I read short stories and fiction (and enough law to teach my courses). I read fiction for pleasure and to find stories and novels to use in my teaching, and I read fiction for what I learn from it. What I discovered as I working on identifying lawyer poets is that poetry too can be read for pleasure and for how and for what it instructs us about the world we inhabit.

Reading poetry, I found poems that amused me and poems that stunned me. Some of the poems arrived like arrows at a target; other poems left me with the image of the archer aiming arrows at the sky, no target in sight. I read poems that had me walking a straight line, and poems that left me feeling like I had wandered into a labyrinth from which the only escape was to set aside the poem. I found poems that were embodiments of mystery. Poetry had finally caught up with me; I was readings poems I thought other lawyers and students of law might want to read.

During this time when I was trying to identify lawyer poets and learning to read poetry, I was editor of the *Legal Studies Forum*, established in the mid-1970s as a humanistic interdisciplinary journal. I invited lawyers to publish their poetry in *LSF*. Most of the poems submitted for publication had nothing to do with law, and I did not solicit or give special attention to law-related poems. I did not subscribe to the idea that a literary legal journal should publish poems related only to law, or poems that only lawyers would be willing to read. In the twelve years that we have published poetry in *LSF*, there has been a steady trickle of poems that focus on lawyers—their lives, their work, their world. These poems were, in my reading, never the lesser work of the poet, and were often quite engaging. In these poems, I began to see the world of legal work as only a poet can see it. The poet and the lawyer, in these lawyer-related poems, had found a way to join worlds we customarily think of as existing indifferent universes.

Contemporary lawyer poets, like lawyer poets throughout history, do not, as a matter of course, draw attention in their poems to their work as lawyers. My library of poetry by lawyers—several thousand volumes—confirms that most lawyer poets do not try to address law or the fact that they are lawyers in their poetry. When lawyers write poems, they are poets, not lawyers; they are poets who happen to be lawyers. Through poetry, they comprehend and animate the world we pass through in silence. And yes, in the long history of lawyer poets, we do find those who have not kept their poetry distant and distinct from their lives as lawyers. The impetus for this anthology lies in the poems of contemporary lawyer poets who were unable or unwilling to maintain a rigid separation between the world they inhabit as lawyers and the world they inhabit as poets.

After paying too little attention to the lawyer-related poems that came my way, I now find that lawyer poets write about the legal world in the same compelling way they do about songbirds, snow storms, winter accidents, and summer love affairs. I have begun to see how the poems written by lawyers—poems about their lives and their work—paint the world in subtle hues we seldom find in other forms of legal writing. The poems collected here make their own best case for an anthology of poetry about lawyers and their work.

Acknowledgments

The poems in this anthology were all selected for publication in the *Legal Studies Forum*, a journal devoted to literary work by and about lawyers. Many of the poems first appeared in literary journals and in collected works by the author, and we want to acknowledge that prior publication of the poems. All poems appear here with the permission of the authors. Bruce Laxalt's poems appear with the permission of his estate.

Richard Bank: Public Defender—Poem #21" first appeared in *Siren's Silence*.

Michael Blumenthal: "This Is It" and "Learning by Doing" appeared in *Days We Would Rather Know* (Viking Press, 1985; Pleasure Boat Studio, 2005); "Letter of Resignation" and "The Metamorphosis" in *Sympathetic Magic* (Watermark Press, 1980); "The Man Who Needed No One" in *Against Romance* (Viking 1985, Pleasure Boat Studio 2006).

M.C. Bruce: "Singing in the Courtroom," "Good Morning," "*Abogado!*" and "The Jury Returns" appeared in *Clients* (Swan Duckling Press, 1998); "The Jury Returns" also appeared in Bruce's chapbook, *26 Sonnets* (Swan Duckling Press, 1999).

James Clarke: The anthology selection of James Clarke poems is drawn from his several collected works of poetry: *Silver Mercies* (Exile Editions, 1997), *The Raggedy Parade* (Exile Editions, 1998), *The Ancient Pedigree of Plums* (Exile Editions 1999), *The Way Everyone Is Inside* (Exile Editions, 2000), *Flying Home Through the Dark* (Exile Editions, 2001), *How to Bribe a Judge: Poems from the Bench* (Exile Editions, 2002), *Forced Passage: A Short History of Hanging* (Exile Editions, 2005), *Dreamworks: New and Selected Poems* (Exile Editions, 2008).

Martín Espada: "The Prisoners of Saint Lawrence," "Sing in the Voice of a God Even Atheists Can Hear," and "Offerings to an Ulcerated God," appeared in Martín Espada, *Imagine the Angels of Bread* (W.W. Norton, 1996). "The Prisoners of Saint Lawrence" was first published in *Rethinking Marxism*; "Sing in the Voice of a God Even Atheists Can Hear" in *Bilingual Review*; "Tires Stacked in the Hallways of Civilization" appeared in *City of Coughing and Dead Radiators* (W.W. Norton & Co., 1993).

Rachel Contreni Flynn: "Slip & Fall" and "Poem on the Road to Depose" appeared in *Ice, Mouth, Song* (Tupelo Press, 2005) .

Nancy Henry: "Baby's First Bath" appeared in Henry's *Anything Can Happen* (MuscleHead Press Chapbooks/Bone World Publishing, 2002); "Wax" was first published in *Ruah* and also appeared in *Who You Are* (Sheltering Pine Press, 2008).

Susan Holahan: "In the Easy Dream" appeared in *Sister Betty Reads the Whole You* (Gibbs-Smith Publisher, 1998) and was first published in *The Plum Review*; "Legal Aid," in a longer version, was first published in the *Minnesota Review*.

Lawrence Joseph: "The Game Changed" appeared in *Into It* (Farrar, Straus & Giroux, 2005); "Curriculum Vitae" is the title poem in *Curriculum Vitae* (University of Pittsburgh Press, 1988) and appeared also in *Codes, Precepts, Biases, and Taboos* (Farrar, Straus & Giroux, 2005).

Richard Krech: "Life on Appeal" appeared in *In Chambers: the Bodhisattva of the Public Defender's Office* (Buffalo, NY: sunnyoutside, 2008).

Bruce Laxalt: All of the Laxalt poems appeared in *Songs of Mourning and Worship* (Black Rock Press, 2005).

David Leightty: "Memo to File" appeared in *Slant* and in *Cumbered Shapes* (Robert L. Barth, 1998); "Constitutionals," "Off the Record," and "The Courthouse Starlings" were also published in *Cumbered Shapes*; "Interpretations" (now part of "Constitutionals") previously appeared in *New Press Literary Quarterly*.

Greg McBride: "After Memo-Writing" first appeared in *WorldWrights!*

James McKenna: The McKenna poems appear in *The Common Law* (Moon Pie Press, 2012).

Joyce Meyers: "Settling on the Eve of Trial" was first published in *Litigation* (a publication of the American Bar Association).

Tim Nolan: "Work" and "Oklahoma" were first published in Tim Nolan's essay, "Poetry and the Practice of Law," in the *South Dakota Law Review*. The essay, in a revised version, is presented as an introduction to the anthology.

Kristen Roedell: "Family Law" was first published in *Workers Write: Tales From the Courtroom* (Blue Cubicle Press, 2011).

Lawrence Russ: "Found Objects" was published in Parker A. Towle's edited collection, *Exquisite Reaction* (Andrew Mountain Press, 2000).

Charles Williams: All of the Williams poems appeared in *Asparagus Seems Deaf* (Harmony House Publishers, 2006).

Kathleen Winter: "In the Clutch" was first published in *Parthenon West Review* and appeared in Vilma Giinzbert & Doug Stout (eds.), *Present at the Creation: An Anthology* (Healdsburg Arts Council, 2006).

The Poets

Lee Wm. Atkinson was born in Detroit, Michigan, in 1949. He attended the University of Michigan, graduating in 1971. He obtained his law degree from the University of Michigan Law School and was admitted to the Bar in 1973. Atkinson worked as an Assistant Attorney General for the State of Michigan, and served as assistant prosecuting attorney in Detroit and chief of the criminal division for the prosecuting attorney's office in Lansing, Michigan. In 1980, he moved to Tampa, Florida, to become an Assistant U.S. Attorney for the Middle District of Florida, where he served as head of the narcotics section and supervised federal drug prosecutions. From 1985 to 1992, Atkinson was Executive Assistant State Attorney in Tampa. After leaving the State Attorney's office, he took up private practice. In addition to his poetry, Atkinson is an accomplished horseman and fencer.

Richard Bank was born in 1942 in Philadelphia. He graduated from Villanova Law School in 1968. In 1972, he joined the Public Defender's office, and later resumed private practice. In 1982, he returned to the Public Defender's office to try major felony cases. Bank also served as an adjunct professor at Villanova Law School where he taught criminal justice. Bank has published two chapbooks: *Some of the Secrets* (Merit Systems, 2002) and *The Drama of Our Species* (Pudding House Press, 2010).

Michael Blumenthal's eighth book of poems, *No Hurry: Poems 2000-2012*, was published by Etruscan Press. A graduate of Cornell Law School and formerly Director of Creative Writing at Harvard, he is the author of the memoir *All My Mothers and Fathers* (Harper Collins, 2002), a novel, *Weinstock Among The Dying* (Pleasure Boat Studio, 2008), and a collection of essays from Central Europe, *When History Enters the House* (Pleasure Boat Studio, 1998). A frequent translator from German, French and Hungarian, he spends summers at his house in a small village near the shores of Lake Balaton in Hungary. In May of 2007, he spent a month in South Africa working with orphaned infant chacma baboons at the C.A.R.E. foundation in Phalaborwa, an experience about which he has written in an upcoming book. He is currently a Visiting Professor of Law at the West Virginia University College of Law, where he has taught since 2009.

Ace Boggess graduated from Marshall University and received his law degree from West Virginia University. His published chapbooks include *Desire's Orchestra* (TLD Press, 1998) and *The Beautiful Girl Whose Wish Was Not Fulfilled* (highwire press, 2003). After his graduation from law school, Boggess devoted himself to literary pursuits and did not undertake the practice of law.

David Bristol was born in 1948, grew up in Verona, New Jersey, and has lived in Arlington, Virginia, for more than three decades. Bristol graduated from New York University and obtained his law degree from George Washington University. He has published three collections of poetry: *The Monk Who Made His Momma Happy* (Bunny and the Crocodile Press, 1977), *Paradise & Cash* (Washington Writers Publishing House, 1980), and *Toad and Other Poems* (Bunny and the Crocodile Press, 2002). Bristol is a staff attorney at the Office of Thrift Supervision, a federal agency under the Department of the Treasury that charters, supervises, and regulates all federally and state chartered savings banks and savings and loans associations.

Lee Warner Brooks was an undergraduate at the University of Michigan, obtained an M.A. from the University of Pennsylvania, and his law degree from the University of Michigan Law School. The author of several novels, Brooks began writing poetry in 2004. His sonnets have appeared in the *Iowa Review, Passager, Light,* and *Poetry in Performance,* and *Novlets,* a special issue of the *Legal Studies Forum.* Brooks has been a cab driver in Ann Arbor, an editor and writer for publishers in Pennsylvania and Maryland, and a partner in the litigation department of a Detroit law firm. Currently, he teaches writing at the University of Michigan in Dearborn.

M.C. Bruce lives in McKinleyville, California, and practices as a solo lawyer. He obtained his J.D. from Berkeley (Boalt Hall). Bruce has worked as a Deputy Public Defender, Supervising Attorney for the Humboldt Alternate Counsel, and associate at a midsized Los Angeles firm. His poems have appeared in *Rattle, Poesy, Urban Spaghetti,* and other journals, as well as in two Orange County, California, poetry anthologies, and in several chapbooks. Bruce edited a small press magazine, *The Blue Mouse,* and served as the original host of KPFK's "The Poet's Café."

Laura Chalar was born in Uruguay in 1976. She graduated as a lawyer in 2001 and holds a postgraduate degree in International Commerical Arbitration. She is the author of a poetry chapbook, *Por así decirlo* (Artefato, 2005) and two short story collections, one of them, *El discreto encanto de la abogací* (Editorial Fin De Siglo, 2007), about lawyers. She is a coordinator, with a fellow writer, of a Uruguayan contemporary poetry blog.

James Clarke was born in Peterborough, Ontario, and attended McGill University and Osgoode Hall. He practiced law in Cobourg, Ontario, before his appointment to the Bench in 1983. Clarke served as a judge of the Superior Court of Ontario and is now retired and resides in Guelph, in southwestern Ontario. Clarke is the author of eight collections of poetry: *Silver Mercies* (Exile Editions, 1997), *The Raggedy Parade* (Exile Editions, 1998), *The Ancient Pedigree of Plums* (Exile Editions, 1999), *The Way Everyone Is Inside* (Exile Editions, 2000), *Flying Home Through the Dark* (Exile Editions, 2001), *How to Bribe a Judge: Poems from the Bench* (Exile Editions, 2002), *Forced Passage: A Short History of Hanging* (Exile Editions, 2005), and *Dreamworks: New and Selected Poems* (Exile Editions, 2008). He is also the author of two memoirs: *A Mourner's Kaddish: Suicide and the Rediscovery of Hope* (Novalis, 2006) and *The Kid from Simcoe Street* (Exile Editions, 2012).

John Crouch was born in 1967 and has lived in Arlington, Virginia, his entire life, except when he attended Brown University and the College of William & Mary, where he obtained his law degree. He practices family law, wills and probate, with an emphasis on international family law. Before he became a lawyer, Crouch worked as a water department laborer, inner-city court-appointed Special Advocate for children, park ranger, legal columnist, and editor.

Martín Espada was born in Brooklyn, New York, in 1957. He grew up in Brooklyn, graduated from Northeastern University Law School in 1985, and became a tenant lawyer, working for six years as a supervisor at *Su Clínica Legal*, a legal services program for low-income, Spanish-speaking tenants in Chelsea, Massachusetts, a program that also served as a clinic for Suffolk University School of Law. Since 1993, Espada has been a professor in the English Department at the University of Massachusetts-Amherst, where he teaches creative writing. Espada's published collections of poetry include *The Immigrant Iceboy's Bolero* (Ghost Pony Press, 1982), *Trumpets From the Islands of Their Eviction* (Bilingual Press, 1987), *Rebellion is the Circle of a Lover's Hands* (Curbstone Press, 1990), *City of Coughing and Dead Radiators* (Norton, 1993), *Imagine the Angels of Bread* (Norton, 1996), *A Mayan Astronomer in Hell's Kitchen* (Norton, 2000), *Alabanza: New and Selected Poems (1982-2002)*

(Norton, 2003), *The Republic of Poetry* (Norton, 2006), *Crucifixion in the Plaza de Armas* (Smokestack Books, 2008), and *The Trouble Ball* (Norton, 2011). Espada is also the author of two essay collections, *Zapata's Disciple: Essays* (South End Press, 1998) and *The Lover of a Subversive Is Also a Subversive: Essays and Commentaries* (University of Michigan Press, 2010).

Rachel Contreni Flynn was born outside Paris, grew up in a small Indiana farming town, and now teaches poetry while serving as a corporate attorney for a Fortune 500 company where she specializes in employment law. She studied at Indiana University and obtained her law degree from Loyola University in Chicago. She received an MFA in poetry from Warren Wilson College in 2001. Her poetry has appeared in *Barrow Street, Florida Review, Epoch, Washington Square, Mississippi Review,* and *Forklift, Ohio.* She is the author of three collections of poetry: *Ice, Mouth, Song* (Tupelo Press, 2005), *Haywire* (Bright Hill Press, 2009), and *Tongue* (Red Hen Press, 2010). She lives in Mundelein, Illinois.

Katya Giritsky was born in Hong Kong of Russian parents who caught the last flight out of Shanghai before the Red Army took the city. She obtained her B.A. in 1970 and her J.D. in 1974 from the University of Southern California. Her poetry has appeared in various journals, and she has published six chapbooks of poetry, three with Swan Duckling Press. She served as a Deputy Public Defender in Orange County, California, and is now retired and living in Seattle, Washington.

Howard Gofreed is an information systems application designer and project manager for an international conglomerate of retail grocery and pharmacy chains. His poetry has appeared in *Negative Capability, The MacGuffin, Lip Service, WordWrights!,* and in Washington, D.C.-area poetry anthologies, including *Cabin Fever* (WordWorks, 2004). He obtained his J.D. from the University of Maryland in 1973.

Nancy Henry was a co-founder, with her law school friend Alice Persons, of Moon Pie Press, a small poetry press. Henry's poems have appeared in *Rattle, Southern Humanities Review, Atlanta Review, Poetry International, The Hollins Critic, Spoon River Poetry Review,* and other publications. She is the author of three poetry collections, *Our Lady of Let's All Sing* (Sheltering Pines Press, 2007), *Who You Are* (Sheltering Pines Press, 2008), and *Sarx* (Moon Pie Press, 2010). Henry has spent most of her career working in child protective law. She is currently an adjunct professor at Central Maine Community College, where she teaches philosophy and communications.

Susan Holahan grew up on Long Island, New York. She received her Ph.D. in English and her J.D. from Yale University. She taught creative writing at Yale College to pay law-school tuition and daycare. Briefly, she worked at New Haven Legal Assistance, then from the late 1970s through the early '90s she taught writing at the University of Rochester. Holahan is the author of a collection of poems, *Sister Betty Reads the Whole You* (Gibbs Smith, 1998). She has also published journalism and short fiction in newspapers, magazines, and books.

Paul Homer wrote his first poetry at age 79 and has since published two collections of poetry: *Neighborhood Legends and Other Poems* (Uptown People's Press, 2004) and *Impressions From a Curmudgeon* (BookSurge Publishing, 2006). At 85, he began writing short stories. Homer served during World War II in an armored reconnaissance battalion in the European theater. After the war, he attended the University of Chicago where he obtained his undergraduate degree, and then Northwestern University, where he obtained his J.D. He became a member of the bar in 1951. Homer, now retired, practiced business, tax, real estate, and commercial law with DLA PIPER, and he maintained a long association with a pro bono storefront legal clinic in Chicago.

Lawrence Joseph was born in Detroit in 1948. He attended the University of Michigan, where he received a B.A. in English Literature in 1970, and the University of Cambridge, where he received a B.A. and an M.A. in English Language and Literature. He then attended the University of Michigan Law School, receiving his J.D. in 1975. After law school, he clerked for Justice G. Mennen Williams of the Michigan Supreme Court, and taught law at the University of Detroit School of Law, before moving to New York City in 1981, where he practiced law with the firm of Shearman & Sterling. He has been a professor of law at St. John's University School of Law in New York City since 1987, teaching courses on labor, employment, torts, and compensation law, legal theory, and jurisprudence. Joseph has published five books of poetry: *Into It* (Farrar, Straus & Giroux, 2005), *Codes, Precepts, Biases, and Taboos: Poems 1973-1993* (Farrar, Straus & Giroux, 2005), *Before Our Eyes* (Farrar, Straus & Giroux, 1993), *Curriculum Vitae* (University of Pittsburgh Press, 1988), and *Shouting at No One* (University of Pittsburgh Press, 1983). Joseph is the author of two books of prose: *Lawyerland* (Farrar, Straus & Giroux, 1997) and *The*

Game Changed: Essays and Other Prose (University of Michigan Press, 2011). Joseph's poetry appears in the current edition of *The Oxford Book of American Poetry*. Law review symposia on his work includes "Some Sort of Chronicler I Am: Narration and the Poetry of Lawrence Joseph" in the *Cincinnati Law Review* and "The Lawyerland Essays" in the *Columbia Law Review*. Joseph has been a member of the board of directors of Poets House, Poetry Society of America, and The Writer's Voice. He now resides in downtown Manhattan.

Kenneth King is a native of Kentucky and taught English at a community college before taking up the study of law in 1995. He obtained his undergraduate degree from Berea College, an M.A. from the University of Kentucky, a Ph.D. from the University of Nebraska, and his J.D. from Vanderbilt in 1998. After law school, King clerked for the Hon. Eugene Siler, Jr., of the U.S. Court of Appeals for the Sixth Circuit; worked as a staff attorney for the Appalachian Research and Defense Fund; and practiced law in Somerset, Kentucky. He has taught writing at colleges and universities in Kentucky, Missouri, and Illinois. He resigned his position as English professor at Western Kentucky University to complete work on his book, *Germs Gone Wild: How the Unchecked Development of Domestic BioDefense Threatens America* (Pegasus, 2010).

John Charles Kleefeld was born in Toronto, Ontario, and lives in Saskatoon, Saskatchewan. He is a law professor at the University of Saskatchewan College of Law. He has also worked as a natural foods chef, baker, economic analyst, and owner of a building maintenance business.

Richard Krech was born in 1946 and grew up in Berkeley, California. He started writing poetry in 1965, and in 1966 founded a short-lived poetry magazine, *The Avalanche*. Krech published several chapbooks under his Undermine Press imprint, and from 1966 to 1969 sponsored weekly poetry readings at a Telegraph Avenue bookstore in Berkeley. Krech's first poetry chapbook was published in 1967, and his poetry has appeared in various small magazines including *Work* (from John Sinclair's Detroit Artists Workshop Press), *Ole, Manhattan Review,* and City Light's *Journal for the Protection of All Beings.* Krech stopped writing poetry in the mid-'70s when he took up the study of law. After graduating from New College of California School of Law, Krech began his criminal defense practice in Oakland in 1980, a practice that involved cases that ranged from shoplifting to murder, trial and appellate work, and pro bono representation of protest demonstrators. Krech started writing poetry again in 2001. His second-generation poems have appeared in *Exit 13*, *Ecstatic Peace Poetry Journal*, *X-Ray*, and *California Defender* (a publication of the California Public Defender's Association), among other magazines and journals.

Bruce Laxalt was born and raised in Reno, Nevada, living two years as a child in southern France. He attended Stanford University, obtaining a degree in philosophy in 1973. After graduating from Stanford Law School in 1976, he worked as a lawyer with the Department of Justice in Washington, D.C., for a year before returning to Nevada to serve as a homicide prosecutor. He later became a civil litigator and established the law firm, Laxalt and Nomura. In 2001, Laxalt was diagnosed with ALS. He continued to practice law both in Nevada and from his home in the Caribbean until his death in 2010. It was after his ALS diagnosis that Laxalt returned to his early love of writing. In 2005, he published *Songs of Mourning and Worship* (Black Rock Press 2005), a book of poems that draws, in part, on his legal cases. In the final years of his life, Laxalt wrote an extensive autobiography, now undergoing editing for publication.

David Leightty is a lawyer in Louisville, Kentucky. He has practiced for more than three and a half decades in the fields of labor, employment, and civil rights. Leightty is the author of *Kentucky Employment and Labor Law* (Data Trace, 1998, with annual updates) and two poetry chapbooks, *Cumbered Shapes* (Robert L. Barth, 1998) and *Civility at the Flood Wall* (Robert L. Barth, 2002). He is also the founder and editor-in-chief of Scienter Press, a small press limited to the publication of poetry. Leightty is a 1977 graduate of the University of Louisville's Brandeis School of Law.

John Levy was born in 1951. He has been with the Pima County Public Defender's Office in Tucson, Arizona, since 1997. His books include *Among the Consonants* (The Elizabeth Press, 1980), *We Don't Kill Snakes Where We Come From: Two Years in a Greek Village* (Querencia Books, 1994), *Oblivion, Tyrants, Crumbs* (First Intensity Press, 2008), and *A Mind's Cargo Shifting: Fictions* (First Intensity Press, 2011). He was a contributing editor to the literary magazine *Madrona* in the 1970s, and in the 1980s worked as a contributing editor to the international literary magazine *Shearsman*.

Greg McBride began writing poems in his mid-fifties while practicing law at the U.S. Department of Transportation, where he served in the Senior Executive Service as Deputy Chief Counsel of the Federal Transit

Administration. His poems, essays, and reviews have appeared in *Chautauqua, Connecticut Review, Gettysburg Review, The Hollins Critic, Poet Lore, Poetry Southeast, Southern Poetry Review, Salmagundi,* and *Roanoke Review.* He graduated from Princeton University in 1967 and obtained his law degree from the Georgetown University Law Center in 1974. McBride, the current and founding editor of *The Innisfree Poetry Journal,* is the author of a chapbook, *Back of the Envelope* (Southeast Missouri State University Press, 2009), and a collection of poetry, *Porthole* (Briery Creek Press, 2012). He is now retired.

James McKenna served as a Maine Assistant Attorney General from 1979 to 2012. In 2010, he was elected to the American Law Institute. McKenna is the author of a collection of poetry titled, *The Common Law* (Moon Pie Press, 2012).

Betsy McKenzie is director of the law library and professor of law at Suffolk University. She is a 1981 law graduate of the University of Kentucky.

Joyce Meyers taught English at the high school and college levels, then practiced law in Philadelphia for nearly three decades, specializing in First Amendment law. She also served for twelve years on the editorial board of *Litigation,* the journal of the Litigation Section of the American Bar Association, and for two years as editor-in-chief. Her poems have appeared in *Comstock Review, Atlanta Review, The Ledge, Iodine Poetry Journal, Slant, The Great American Poetry Show, Common Ground Review,* and *Mad Poets Review.* She has published two chapbooks, *Wild Mushrooms* (Plan B Press, 2007) and *Shapes of Love* (Finishing Line Press, 2010).

Jesse Mountjoy is a native of Horse Cave, Kentucky, a 1965 graduate of Centre College of Danville, Kentucky, and a 1969 graduate of Vanderbilt University School of Law. After being admitted to the bar in 1970, he served a four-year stint as senior trial attorney for the Internal Revenue Service, where he tried cases in the U.S. Tax Court. After working with the IRS, Mountjoy moved to Owensboro, Kentucky, where he has practiced tax law in the same firm for over thirty years. Mountjoy's poetry has been published in *Open 24 Hours, Wind Magazine, The Sow's Ear Poetry Review, Kentucky Poetry Review, Approaches, Adena,* and *The Small Pond Magazine of Literature.*

Tim Nolan was born in Minneapolis in 1954. He graduated from the University of Minnesota in 1978 and, with his wife, moved to New York City where he obtained an MFA from Columbia University, worked as an archivist at the Whitney Museum, and read the poetry slush pile for *Paris Review*. He returned to Minnesota in 1985, received his J.D. degree from William Mitchell College of Law in 1989, and took up the practice of law. Nolan is currently in solo practice in Minneapolis focusing on commercial and real estate litigation. His poetry has appeared in *The Nation, Ploughshares,* and *Poetry East.* Garrison Keillor has read his poems on *The Writer's Almanac* on National Public Radio.

Simon Perchik was born in 1923 in Paterson, New Jersey. He is a graduate of New York University, where he received both his B.A. in English and his law degree. Perchik, a pilot during World War II, was awarded the Distinguished Flying Cross, among other military decorations. He was admitted to the New York Bar in 1951 and worked primarily in a private law practice, except for five years when he was Assistant District Attorney for Suffolk County, New York. Perchik has published twenty chapbooks and collections of poetry, including: *I Counted Only April: First Poems* (Elizabeth Press, 1964), *Twenty Years of Hands* (Elizabeth Press, 1966), *Which Hand Holds the Brother: Poems 1966-1968* (Elizabeth Press, 1969), *Hands You Are Secretly Wearing* (Elizabeth Press, 1972), *Both Hands Screaming* (Elizabeth Press, 1975), *The Club Fits Either Hand* (Elizabeth Press, 1979), *Mr. Lucky* (Shearsman Books, 1984), *Who Can Touch These Knots: New and Selected Poems* (Scarecrow Press, 1985), *The Gandolf Poems* (White Pine Press, 1988), *The Snowcat Poems* (Linwood Publishers, 1989), *Redeeming the Wings* (Dusty Dog Chapbook Series, 1991), *The Emptiness Between My Hands* (Dusty Dog Press, 1992), *Letters to the Dead* (St. Andrews Press, 1993), *These Hands Filled With Numbness* (Dusty Dog Press, 1996), *Touching the Headstone* (Stride Publication, 2000), and *The Autochthon Poems* (Split/Shift, 2001). The most comprehensive collection of Perchik's poetry can be found in *Hands Collected 1949-1999* (Pavement Saw Press, 2000). Perchik resides in East Hampton, New York.

Carl Reisman has a solo practice of law in Champaign-Urbana, Illinois. He is the author of two poetry collections, *Kettle* (Hot Lead Press, 2005) and *Home Geography* (Stone City Press, 2008). Reisman organized and led the first symposium celebrating the poetry of lawyers, cosponsored by the University of Illinois College of Law and the University of Illinois MFA Creative Writing Program, which took place during a Valentine's week blizzard in Urbana, Illinois, in 2007.

Charles Reynard serves as a Circuit Court Judge in Central Illinois. His poems have appeared on WGLT Public Radio's "Poetry Radio," in the anthology *Where We Live: Illinois Poets* (Greatunpublished, 2003, edited by Kathleen Kirk), and in literary journals, including *AfterHours, Apocalypse,* and *Crab Orchard Review,* as well as in the *National Catholic Reporter.* Reynard is the author of a chapbook, *The Utility of Heart Break* (Pikestaff Press, 2010) and co-author, with Judith Valente, of *Twenty Poems to Nourish Your Soul* (Loyola Press, 2006).

Steven M. Richman practices international commercial law. He has served on the editorial boards of the *New Jersey Lawyer Magazine* and the *New Jersey Law Journal,* and in the House of Delegates of the American Bar Association. Richman is the author of scholarly essays on the lawyer poets Edgar Lee Masters, Sidney Lanier, William Cullen Bryant, and Charles Reznikoff. Richman's poetry has been published in various literary journals and appears in the anthology *American Poetry Confronts the 1990s* (Black Tie Press, 1991). Richman is a photographer whose work is held in various private and public collections. He is also the author of *The Bridges of New Jersey: Portraits of Garden State Crossings* (Rutgers University Press, 2005), *Mannequins* (Schiffer Books, 2005), *The Great Swamp: New Jersey's National Treasure* (Schiffer Publishing, 2008), and *Reconsidering Trenton: The Small City in the Industrial Age* (McFarland Publishers, 2010).

Lee Robinson practiced law in South Carolina for over twenty years and was the first female president of the Charleston Bar Association. She now lives on a ranch in the Texas hill country and teaches at the Center for Medical Humanities and Ethics, University of Texas Health Science Center, in San Antonio. Robinson's first collection of poetry, *Hearsay,* was published by Fordham University Press in 2004, and a second collection, *Creed,* was published by Plainview Press in 2009. She is also the author of *Gateway* (Houghton Mifflin, 1996), a young adult novel about a custody case.

Kristen Roedell is a Northwest poet and retired attorney. She graduated from Whitman College in 1984 and obtained her J.D. from the University of Washington Law School in 1987. She practiced family, criminal, and personal injury law in several Pacific Northwest jurisdictions. She began submitting her poetry for publication in 2009 and her work has now appeared in over fifty journals and anthologies, including *Switched on Gutenberg, Journal of the American Medical Association, Santa Fe Literary Review,* and *Sierra Nevada Review.* She is the author of two collections of poetry: *Seeing in the Dark*

(Tomato Can Press, 2009) and *Girls With Gardenias* (Flutter Press, 2011).

Barbara B. Rollins served as a Texas judge presiding over misdemeanors, small civil cases, juveniles, and probate. In 2007, joining several friends, she became a partner in Silver Boomer Books, a publishing company based in Abilene, Texas. Rollins has written several books drawing on poetry and has for several decades worked on a history of pioneer women judges of Texas.

Lawrence Russ has served since 1986 as an Assistant Attorney General for the State of Connecticut. From 1986 to 1990, he served as Chairman of the Connecticut Bar Association's Committee on Arts and the Law, and from 1986 to 1989 as Director of the annual Connecticut Arts Law Conference. Russ received an MFA from the University of Massachusetts, Amherst. His poems and prose have appeared in *The Nation*, *New York Quarterly*, *Iowa Review*, *Virginia Quarterly Review*, *Parabola*, *Chelsea*, *Image*, and in various anthologies. He received an Artist Fellowship in Poetry from the Connecticut Commission for the Arts. Russ is also an art photographer.

Michael Sowder is an English professor at Utah State University. He received his Ph.D. from the University of Michigan, an M.F.A. from Georgia State University, and his J.D. from the University of Washington; his undergraduate work was at the University of Alabama. After obtaining his law degree, Sowder clerked for a federal judge and practiced law in Atlanta before becoming an English professor. Sowder is the author of three collections of poems: *The Empty Boat* (Truman State University Press, 2004), *A Calendar of Crows* (New Michigan Press, 2001), and *Cafe Midnight* (Blue Scarab Press, 2003, with Margaret Aho). His critical study of Walt Whitman, *Whitman's Ecstatic Union: Conversion and Ideology in Leaves of Grass*, was published by Routledge in 2005.

Ann Tweedy grew up in a small town in Massachusetts. She has been writing poetry since she moved to the West Coast in 1996 to attend law school at Boalt Hall. Her poems have appeared in *Clackamas Literary Review*, *Rattle*, *Avocet*, *Harrington Lesbian Fiction Quarterly*, *Berkeley Poetry Review*, and *The Awakenings Review*. After working for an Indian tribe in rural Washington, she took up teaching and is now on the law faculty at Hamline University.

Charles Williams, a graduate of Duke University and the University of Kentucky College of Law, practices law in Munfordville, Kentucky. His first collection of poetry, *Asparagus Seems Deaf*, was published by Harmony House

Publishers in 2006. He is also the author of a chapbook, *The Trees of Life: Poetry from West Wind Tree Farm* (CDW, 2010). On his West Wind Farm, Williams has undertaken conservation and forest ecosystem work that received recognition from the Kentucky Division of Forestry, the American Forest Foundation, and the Arbor Day Foundation. In 2011, he was nominated for National Tree Farmer of the Year.

Kathleen Winter graduated from the University of California-Davis School of Law, and clerked for the Honorable George H. King, a Federal District Court judge. She practiced land use law in Northern California until 2008, when she entered the MFA Creative Writing program at Arizona State University, graduating in 2011. Winter also holds M.A. and B.A. degrees in English Literature from Boston College and the University of Texas at Austin. Winter's poetry collection, *Nostalgia for the Criminal Past*, was published by Elixir Press in 2012. Winter's poems have appeared in *The New Republic*, *Tin House*, *Field*, *AGNI*, *Cincinnati Review*, *New American Writing*, and *Barrow Street*. Winter currently teaches literature, public speaking, and writing at the University of San Francisco and Napa Valley College.

Warren Wolfson served as an Illinois judge for over thirty years, first on the Cook County Circuit Court, and then on the Illinois Appellate Court. He resigned from the bench in 2009 to serve as interim dean of the DePaul University College of Law.

Author Index

CPSIA information can be obtained
at www.ICGtesting.com
Printed in the USA
FSOW02n1156281114
3608FS